Positive Financial Karma

Daniel J. Geltrude

Cover Artwork by Bill Lopa

Back Cover Photo by Alexander Wenkel

Printed in the United States of America
First Printing, 2019
ISBN: 978-0-578-41957-2

DAN GELTRUDE

Delivering Positive Financial Karma

About the Author
Daniel J. Geltrude

Dan Geltrude, known as "America's Accountant" and the "Finance Guru," delivers his unique brand of financial common sense to his clients and as a frequent guest expert on Fox News, CBS and NBC, to name just a few outlets. A business owner and college professor, he is also a longtime radio voice. A gifted communicator, Dan was the commencement speaker at his college graduation at Rider University, where he received his Bachelor's Degree in Accounting.

The author founded Geltrude & Company, LLC in 1995, and cultivated it from sole practitioner to a leading accounting and financial consulting firm located just outside Manhattan. Dan is a Certified Public Accountant and business consultant who specializes in serving real estate developers, successful entrepreneurs, privately owned businesses and wealthy families. He has a Master's Degree in Taxation from Fairleigh Dickinson University and a Master's Degree in Human Resources and Employment Relations from Penn State University.

Positive Financial Karma is Dan's first book, covering a range of topics that will be familiar to his business and personal clients and the countless viewers and listeners who follow him in the national media.

For more information about Dan, visit www.DanGeltrude.com and www.Geltrude.com. Also follow Dan on Twitter at @DanGeltrude.

About the Artist
Bill Lopa

Bill Lopa has been the Official Commemorative Artist of the Super Bowl, World Series, Major League baseball All-Star game and Kentucky Derby. He has been commissioned by celebrities including Michael Jordan, Derek Jeter, Barbara Sinatra, Mariano Rivera and Peyton Manning.

Lopa's artwork has been featured in galleries across the country. His paintings have helped raise money for the American Cancer Society, Barbara Sinatra Children's Center, Klein Family Learning Center, Jockeys' Guild, James Graham Brown Cancer Center, the Leukemia Foundation and the V Foundation for Cancer Research.

Some of his work can be found at www.LopaStudios.com.

Cover Art
Interpretation

Bill Lopa has captured the essence of Positive Financial Karma with his dazzling painting of Wall Street. We see the bull and bear battling for control of the stock market, while Dan Geltrude rises upon scaffolding in deep meditation. Ultimately, the bull and bear will submit to the positive intention radiating through the fervent meditation of the "Finance Guru."

Dedication

Four people above all others have had a profound impact on my life: my grandparents. They provided me with unconditional love, encouragement, protection – and great food. They sacrificed so much for my benefit and instilled in me the notion that all things are possible. There isn't a day that passes when I don't think of them. So it is with a heavy heart and deep gratitude that I dedicate this book to them.

Cosimo Damiano Geltrude

Anna Spadaro Geltrude

John Verrico

Filomena Basile Verrico

At the moment when our paths cross again, only then will my grieving finally end.

"Young people need something stable to hang on to —
a culture connection, a sense of their own past,
a hope for their own future. Most of all, they need
what grandparents can give them."
– Jay Kesler

"Nothing is free.

You pay with currency, time or karma."

– Daniel J. Geltrude

Table of Contents

When Politicians Strike

When Consumers Fight Back

Karma and Your Finances: The Basics

Introduction:
My Road to Karma

Aside from my years away at college, I have always resided in Nutley, New Jersey. More than anything else, I feel safe here. The majority of people in this community are Italian and Roman Catholic. Perhaps I only had to say Italian because being Catholic is a given for Italians. Although the town has become more ethnically diverse over the years, it still has a significant Italian-American presence.

While I have always identified strongly with my Italian heritage, I have never felt comfortable in church. In fact, growing up I fought my parents tooth and nail about going to church or religious study. Even as an adult, I never warmed up to the idea.

When my father died in 2006 after a year-long battle with melanoma, I searched for answers as to why it happened. I understand that cancer kills millions of people around the world each year. But why did it happen to him?

I believe it's quite common for people to turn to their religious faith for answers after losing a loved one. But I never had a strong faith in anything religion-based and I instinctively knew that church wasn't where I would find my answers. I wanted to find something that made sense to me. So it had to be logic-based, not religion- or faith-based.

Maybe it was just my father's karma to die of cancer, I thought. That made some sense to me, even though I didn't initially understand why. As I thought more about his death, these facts became clear:

- My father spent a lot of time in the sun;
- Sun exposure causes skin cancer;
- The doctors didn't catch it in time;
- So, melanoma killed him.

In other words, there was "cause and effect" related to his situation. I needed to understand this more, which ultimately led me to study Buddhism, where cause and effect is an integral part of the philosophy. I started by reading books. Then I sought out people with the most knowledge I could find to learn more.

There is a saying attributed to the Buddha which states, *"When a student is ready, the teacher will appear."* I have had the great fortune of being in the presence of, and receiving teachings from, two of the greatest Buddhist teachers in the world: His Holiness the 14th Dalai Lama, and the venerable Thich Nhat Hanh. In addition, I learned much from such teachers as Khyongla Rato Rinpoche, Thubten Zopa Rinpoche, Nicholas Vreeland and Elliot Negron Black (aka Ekesvara Shiva Baba). Each of them has opened my mind on multiple levels to Buddhist philosophy and teachings. Additionally, the weekly teachings and studies offered at The Tibet Center in Manhattan and South Orange, NJ have been invaluable.

The Dalai Lama once said *"Don't use Buddhism to become a Buddhist. Use Buddhism to become better at whatever else in your life you are doing already."*

This is what I have decided to do.

Although I sometimes say I am a Buddhist just to keep things simple, I prefer not to be labeled at all. For me, Buddhism is not about religion, but about trying to achieve better outcomes in every aspect of life. With that in mind, this book will focus on one aspect of life that I practice here in the present – providing financial advice.

There are many books about Buddhism and there are many books about achieving positive financial outcomes. To my knowledge, there are few that combine the two. This book is not intended to convert you to Buddhism. Instead, my intent is to expose you to a different way of approaching finances and to provide the tools you need to achieve successful outcomes on multiple levels.

Eat Less,
Move More

It might seem odd that you chose this book to learn how to achieve Positive Financial Karma and one of the first things you see is a chapter titled, "Eat Less, Move More."

Say what? What do diet and exercise have to do with money? In this scenario, a "less-and-more" combination will create a healthier you, potentially leading to fewer costly medical bills. When your goal is to eat less and exercise more, and you follow through on your intention with action, you may actually create Positive Financial Karma.

So, if we want to lose weight, we all know the answer. Eat less and move more. Assuming you have no health or medical issues and you hold yourself accountable, you WILL lose weight.

The same holds true for spending and saving. If you intend to spend less and save more and you hold yourself accountable, you WILL create Positive Financial Karma.

See the connection?

Nothing in this book is complicated. You already know the solutions to many of life's challenges, and you understand that they start with intention that leads to action. Ultimately, every one of our actions creates some type of reaction.

As a professor, I find that students achieve the highest level of learning by taking a hands-on approach. By deciding to read this book, you've taken action to learn about producing Positive Financial Karma, and I hope it will inspire you to react by committing to the work required to better your financial life.

Let's get started.

What Goes Around
Comes Around

What exactly is karma?

It begins with a thought.

A thought will evolve into intention. I intend to create financial security for myself and my family. That's positive intent.

Next, determine the action you need to take. I need to spend less and save more.

Finally, hold yourself accountable for taking the needed action. I will allocate dollars toward my goals. I know that saving nothing is also an action, but not a positive one.

When you diligently take these actions you will create Positive Financial Karma. In this case, karma is the effect or outcome of your actions.

You can achieve individual karma and community karma – the latter, for example, when you vote for your elected officials.

Think of karma as a boomerang: What goes around comes around. We all know the phrase "karma is a bitch," when we feel someone had it coming. Karma can be good or bad. A drug dealer can make lots of money, but his karma will most certainly not be positive.

While Positive Financial Karma may result from positive intent and action – obtaining more education, working overtime, starting a business – it isn't simply about making more money. Again, I use the drug dealer as an example. His karma is clearly bad because his intent is horrible and the societal results are horrendous. It doesn't matter how rich the dealer becomes.

Conversely, if you intend to become a civil engineer in order to make our roads and bridges safer, your outcome will likely be a sizable dose of Positive Financial Karma because you had nothing but good intentions. Work hard to advance in virtually any legitimate career in order to take better care of your family and/or do good for the greater community and you'll create Positive Financial Karma.

Because karma can take time, you may not see it immediately. But with positive intent and action, Positive Financial Karma will happen, whether it takes months to lose weight to achieve individual karma or a lifetime to change government's reckless spending habits to achieve community karma.

Our goals aren't always easy to achieve. Yet, good intentions can keep us focused throughout our lives, turning into positive action when we take responsibility. The effect, or outcome, is what we make of it: We drop the pounds or we don't. We save for retirement or we don't.

Throughout this book, you can use "Eat Less, Move More" as a figurative guide to finding Positive Financial Karma. I'll show you how to achieve it, even in the most unlikely circumstances. Then it's up to you to turn positive intentions into actions that will get you there.

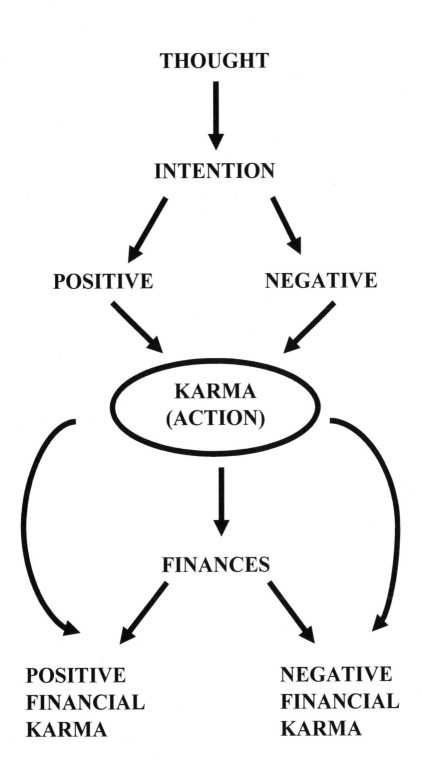

Tax and Tax Again

Raising Taxes Bad,
Cutting Taxes Good

Need I say more?

OK, I'll say just a little bit more about the subject.

I'm not heartless. Money can accomplish many positive things.
It can feed poor families who are unable to feed themselves.
It can provide medical care to our veterans, the very least they
deserve from us. Money should protect our most vulnerable
and our country.

But very often it goes elsewhere.

Lawmakers' intentions rarely turn into long-lasting initiatives.
Local and federal governments divert – or steal – funds. Programs
become bloated and politicians with decidedly bad karma abuse
them. Government often tells us it knows better than we do. And
politicians keep the pork-barrel express humming along. Positive
Financial Karma this ain't.

I believe we should keep more of our own money in our own pockets because we know better than government – a lot better, and it
will improve taxpayers' prospects for Positive Financial Karma.

Once when I appeared on a national cable television news network
to discuss taxes, the producer said through my earpiece, "We need

to break so be very short with your response." So when the host asked what my view of tax cuts was, I simply said: "Raising taxes bad, cutting taxes good."

Need I say more?

Spend, Spend, Spend –
Owe, Owe, Uh-Oh!

You may have heard that the total debt of the United States has passed $21 trillion.

That's 21 . . . TRILLION . . . dollars . . . and counting!

How did our national debt reach such astronomical heights? Let's start by looking at the federal budget passed at the beginning of 2018. With this bill, ridiculously named the Bipartisan Budget Act of 2018, Congress approved a budget of $1.21 trillion, while enacting ZERO spending cuts and adding another trillion, give or take a few billion, to the federal debt. Is this a bad joke? I wish it was, but unfortunately it is not.

While we run up mind-boggling debt, Congress crows about bipartisanship. It's easy to be bipartisan when everybody gets what they want. But this is not compromise, which is what happens when you get something but you also give something up.

This bloated budget is on top of the tax cuts enacted at the end of 2017, which may add another $1 trillion or more in debt, depending on the extent to which lowering taxes and decreasing regulations play a role. At least the tax cuts have the potential to spur economic growth, which could increase tax revenues and reduce the projected debt.

But getting back to the latest budget, you need to know this was an outrageous 13 percent increase over the previous year's budget.

It was $143 billion more than President Trump even asked for, and it was more than either the Democrats or Republicans requested. In other words, everyone got the chance to run up the federal credit card and stick the next generation of taxpayers with the bill.

So, how do we pay down exploding national debt?

We don't, just as we haven't done for the past several years. We spend, spend, spend and we owe, owe, owe.

Until we fall off the financial cliff.

Pity our children and grandchildren.

In April 2018, the Congressional Budget Office (CBO) projected how the federal debt would continue to increase over the next decade. The debt has doubled in the past 10 years as a percentage of gross domestic product (GDP), and will approach 100 percent of GDP by 2028, according to the CBO's projections.

In other words, we would need to use every tax dollar generated by individuals and companies in this country to pay off our national debt.

Not that any of this bothers our elected representatives. They spend money like they can just print more of it (and they can). The worst kind of fool couldn't spend like this. It's an exercise in a new and unimaginable level of irresponsibility. This is crazy.

Really crazy.

On top of all this, in early 2018 the president talked about spending another $200 billion or so on infrastructure improvements. This may or may not materialize by the time you read this, and you can argue that the economic benefits might somewhat offset the added expense. But it won't be enough. So there is plenty of blame to go around. This is about reckless fiscal policies. This level of debt is not sustainable.

Our country will fall – no, sprint – off the financial cliff unless the economy grows at much higher levels than we have seen in decades AND we make significant spending cuts. The problem is that members of Congress will not make hard decisions, at least not as long as their priority remains re-election.

Granted, we have to spend money to ensure our national security and to secure programs that help the elderly, the sick and those who truly need assistance. There are, however, countless other areas where tremendous waste could be cut. But few of our elected officials are brave enough to introduce or vote for budget cuts because doing so could potentially cost them their seats in office.

Who in their right mind would spend money blindly and never worry about the cost? Who would always buy the most expensive thing without even a second thought? Our elected officials would. Our elected officials often make the wrong decisions because they are more concerned with winning re-election.

More than conservativism or liberalism, politicians of all stripes mostly follow one specific ideology – re-electionism (yes, I made up that word). That's why governments seldom achieve Positive Financial Karma. They neither achieve it nor distribute it to taxpayers.

I am extremely concerned about where our nation is heading because at some point the bill will come due and I don't know how we will repay it — and increased taxes can only get you so far.

In my home state of New Jersey I believe we've already reached a tax brick wall, as corporations and wealthy individuals continue their exodus. Nationally, you only need to look at the federal debt and you'll find 21 trillion reasons to back my theory. The astounding thing about our increasing debt is that tax revenues, at least nationally, are actually rising, but we're spending more and more – above and beyond whatever taxes Congress puts in place.

The result is that even when our elected officials vote for well-intentioned spending, government inevitably creates negative financial karma because the debt keeps getting bigger.

The only way to erase this negativity and ease these doomsday debt levels is to oust the offenders from political office – sooner rather than later. There are few other solutions. Voting for and demanding fiscal sanity is one way voters can achieve Positive Financial Karma on a large scale. Another way is to demand term limits, a theme you will see repeated throughout this book.

With term limits and without the need to placate voters to win re-election, politicians might actually exhibit the political courage they need to make the hard decisions that will save America from plunging off the financial cliff.

Meanwhile, we edge closer and closer and closer . . .

Pension Obligations

While $21 trillion in federal debt rightly attracts a lot of attention, states around the country are also drowning in their own seas of debt. One of the primary causes of this growing fiscal crisis is a failure to keep up with rising public-employee pension obligations – among the biggest reasons for this growing mound of debt.

A study released in 2018 by the Pew Charitable Trusts found that state pension liabilities in 2016 grew to a staggering $1.4 trillion – that's trillion – dollars. This was a $295 billion increase in just one year. As bad as mounting pension liabilities are all over the country, imagine how much worse the situation will be when the stock market experiences a correction. Talk about negative financial karma!

As it stands today, only Wisconsin has come close to fully funding its public pensions, with three other states funding at least 90 percent of their pension commitments. Almost half of the states funded two-thirds or less of their pension obligations. Two states, including my home state of New Jersey, funded just 31 percent of obligations.

This is ridiculous. Consumers can't commit to paying full price for something and then say, "tough luck," and pay just 31 percent of the cost. That's what New Jersey and other states in similar straits may have to do if they don't get their financial acts together yesterday.

It won't be long before the biggest offenders have unmanageable amounts of pension debt pushing them off the financial cliff and forcing them into bankruptcy. And the bill will come due. No matter how hard politicians might try, they can't tax us at 120 percent of income, yet they won't cut spending because fiscal irresponsibility is the easy response.

In today's environment, there is no solution except – and tell me if you've heard this before – we either vote the offenders out of office or demand term limits. Your ability to achieve Positive Financial Karma depends on this.

If we put politicians in place who actually make the hard decisions needed to remedy the immediate fiscal problem, then a workable solution that doesn't break the backs of taxpayers can finally be achieved.

Already, some municipalities are trying new solutions by switching from defined benefit pensions – which are the typical guaranteed pensions in trouble today – to defined contribution plans, such as 401(k) plans, for new employees. Existing employees are typically grandfathered in their traditional pension plans so they needn't worry about losing their benefits.

Unless, of course, the states don't pay their bills.

With a 401(k) plan, which most corporations have, employees are responsible for how much they contribute (up to limits) and they make their own investment decisions. So-called automatic tools for savings and asset allocation combined with a good dose of investment education could help employees make appropriate choices, which is important because this type of retirement plan offers few guarantees.

The ideal solution would see politicians immediately reform their pension bad habits, then work toward an overall fiscal policy that stresses cutting spending over raising taxes.

States can't print their own money and they can't tax their way out of this problem. Until they realize this, their financial karma looks bad.

Will politicians see the light? I doubt it. Without term limits, they will continue to roll the dice and we taxpayers will continue to pay the price.

Soda Tax

There are countless examples of taxes that are nothing more than government money grabs. In virtually every case, the money that we thought was earmarked for a noble cause simply ended up in government's pockets, directed to ever-growing, never-ending crusades allegedly designed to save us from ourselves. So, I begin my measured response to the latest craze – Big Government's quest to save us from the ill effects of soda and other sugary drinks.

I am a big proponent of healthy living and I am convinced most of us can do many things, including staying away from sugary drinks, to live healthier lives. Reducing sugar is surely a noble cause – a good intention – and, I would imagine, a benefit to our health. But taxes on soda and other sugary drinks are little more than taxes disguised as a health incentive.

Even avowed tax-lover Sen. Bernie Sanders voiced opposition to the tax because of its disproportionate effect on low-income families. Let me count the flaws in the soda tax and similar sin taxes and describe how they hurt the poor and eventually everyone else.

1. These types of taxes are designed to influence individual behavior and actions. So I say, "OK, that's one more thing government thinks it can do better than me and one more individual responsibility to take from us." Still, the initial idea is a good intention.

2. Legislators who don't want people consuming sugary drinks or tobacco seem to think taxing the items heavily means people will not be able or willing to afford them. This sounds great in theory except human nature tells us that many, including lower-income people, will continue to find a way to support these habits despite the increased cost.

3. I would agree that soda contributes to obesity, diabetes and other health issues. But wouldn't you think that politicians should use all the tax money - not some of the money, but ALL of the money – to develop programs that address sugar-related health conditions? They don't.

4. This is where good intentions go to die. You can almost count on government using less of the tax money for its initial purpose over time until it uses none of it as originally intended. In the end, the funds collected simply become a drop in the bucket to fight higher and higher budget deficits.

Here's the thing: I don't know a person who doesn't want to see type II diabetes and heart disease wiped out. But I believe that government will eventually divert the money appropriated to these and other issues elsewhere. Look at Cook County in Illinois, whose Board of Commissioners voted 9-to-8 to institute a soda tax but repealed the wildly unpopular law a year later by a 15-to-1 vote. The reason: The money was going to plug budget deficits, not address the health problems — plus it didn't raise the intended revenue because border residents drove to Indiana for their sugary drinks.

What a shock!

Ask yourself this: Would government really be happy if everyone swore off sugary drinks and the coffers from the sugary drink tax ran dry?

Just saying.

Think not only about the intention, but the guarantees from government that ALL the taxes collected from alcohol, tobacco, sugary drinks, gasoline and marijuana go toward drunken driving awareness, smoking cessation, healthy living initiatives, new roads and bridges and pain management programs.

While you ponder where the soda tax might eventually wind up, you can at least take solace in the knowledge that avoiding soda taxes and living a healthier life as a result make for Positive Financial Karma.

Plastic Bag Tax

Taxing soda and other sugary drinks is only one of the ways our elected officials take money from us. Taxing plastic bags is the latest way government has devised to raise its revenues — directly from consumers.

Don't get me wrong. I'm all for ridding the world of plastics. They take centuries to degrade and are a danger to our environment and wildlife. But there is always a better solution than taxing something out of existence. As we have found with taxes on soda, cigarettes and alcohol, government's claim of positive intent to fix a problem through taxation quickly becomes our problem in the form of more state and national debt.

There are issues you need to consider before you can make an informed decision about a plastics tax. If you are a business owner – let's say a supermarket owner who depends on cost-efficient plastic bags – you will bear the cost of providing more expensive alternatives if the bags are banned. If you are a consumer, you will pay more at the market for plastic bags or you will need to bring reusable bags with you.

The plastic bags that stores now sell for reuse are not yet biodegradable, which presents an environmental problem when they eventually wear out from use. Cloth bags are a better alternative, but both types of bags can create foodborne illnesses if not cleaned properly, and who has the time for this extra work?

You might wonder, "Why not use paper bags when most supermarkets hand them out for free?" Free is a relative term, because even paper presents its own environmental concerns. And have you ever tried walking home holding paper bags filled at the supermarket? I challenge you to do so without having half the bags tear and spill groceries into the gutter!

Government could solve this problem and help develop bags that are both biodegradable and strong, but that's wishful thinking. Instead, our politicians tax the cheap plastic bags we now use. As a result, I am pretty pessimistic about a solution because I expect – as in other cases – government will eventually spend the additional tax revenue elsewhere.

Our politicians could defy all precedent and fix the problem – and they would certainly get Positive Financial Karma for slowing the damage to our environment. But taxing plastic out of existence is the wrong action to take. Families at the lower end of the economic spectrum didn't have the five cents a bag New York City imposed on plastic bags a while back – negative financial karma for these families, for sure, and they certainly didn't have the disposable income to buy reusable bags.

New York City clergy spoke out against this tax and its impact on working families, prompting New York Gov. Andrew Cuomo to block the law in 2017. He did, however, introduce a bill for a statewide plastic bag ban starting in 2019. Which brings us back to the alternative of paper, which isn't sturdy enough, or reusable bags, which are prone to creating foodborne illnesses when not cleaned properly.

Sometimes I daydream and wonder, "Hey, here's a radical idea. Wouldn't it be great if government helped create an affordable sturdy, biodegradable plastic bag?" Business benefits. Consumers benefit. The environment benefits.

Then I snap back to reality, knowing that government will take this tax revenue and use it to create ever-growing federal programs without input from voters that will once again increase the behemoth that is government debt.

I predict a company in the private sector will ultimately develop a product that will solve this problem. This company will rightfully reap the financial rewards and positive karma related to the environment. But don't be surprised if the government finds a way to tax it!

"Higher" Taxes

Sometimes you can see the forest through the weed.

While you can't tax taxpayers until there is nothing left to tax, you can legalize and tax marijuana at levels partakers might otherwise balk at if applied to other products – if states where it is legal are any indicators.

I'm making no moral judgment here. I also don't have the expertise to opine on whether marijuana is a gateway drug. My gut instinct tells me it all depends on the propensities of the individual.

What is clear is that legal marijuana sales are becoming the next big cash cow for cash-strapped state governments. A growing number of states and the District of Columbia allow marijuana sales to recreational users, while most states permit medical marijuana sales.

Legal marijuana sales are predicted to reach $25 billion by 2021. While smoking marijuana recreationally won't likely produce Positive Financial Karma, taxing a growing legal market for it will certainly give unrestrained government a tax revenue karma of sorts.

The nonprofit Tax Foundation notes that Washington (the state) socks marijuana users with a 37 percent sales tax, while Massachusetts adds an excise tax of 10.75 percent on top of its normal sales tax rate. Nevada and Colorado levy both sales and excise taxes on the weed, too, totaling 25 percent and 30 percent respectively.

California and Alaska tax marijuana growers, with the latter charging $50 per ounce. Growers pass this cost on to users, who thus far aren't complaining about price.

States aren't complaining, either. California, for one, expects marijuana taxes to create a large impact on tax revenue. In 2018, the state expected an additional $643 million in tax revenue, with future estimates topping $1 billion annually.

There is a small chance growth in this new legal industry can stop cold turkey. As of this writing, the federal government was threatening to crack down on legal sales in these states, citing a federal law against the production, sale and use of marijuana. I think it is unreasonable to be against medical marijuana to help the suffering, and most Americans believe marijuana should be legal for recreational use.

Again, I offer no moral judgment. Perhaps making pot legal is equivalent to legal drinking. That also means that driving under the influence and abusing pot will become a bigger problem, and the financial and other costs to society remain to be seen.

But as a revenue source, marijuana is the "it" item of the day. Even former U.S. House of Representatives' Speaker John Boehner, a Republican, is a convert. Once a die-hard opponent, Boehner has joined the advisory board of one of the leading marijuana-producing companies in the country. Talk about sparking it up for the marijuana industry!

Still, I fear the marijuana tax, like the other taxes mentioned here, will feed the insatiable appetite of government. Eventually, we will end up in the same place – looking for new things to tax. What do they say about the definition of insanity – doing the same thing over and over and expecting a different outcome? Well, this is insanity!

On an individual level, investing in marijuana-related companies is, I guess, on par with investing in alcohol producers, if not first among equals because of its medicinal benefits. Whether owning marijuana stocks results in your personal Positive Financial Karma will depend on how you view the product.

I have no doubt that we'll see more states legalize weed and partake in the tax windfall. It will, however, take a while before we see the fiscal benefits and job creation the industry promises.

In any event, legal marijuana is on the way and will be here to stay once politicians get hooked on the tax revenues it generates and the corresponding government spending that will follow.

For Whom
the Road Tolls

Early in 2018, President Trump floated the idea of a 25-cents-a-gallon diesel and gasoline tax to pay for infrastructure spending. U.S. Transportation Secretary Elaine Chao also talked up a federal gas tax as one way to pay for infrastructure improvements.

If you've read the previous chapters, you won't be surprised to learn that my first reaction to this proposal was that it wasn't a great idea. But you might be surprised that I thought it was necessary, given the terminal inability of government to cut spending. We have to come up with something because infrastructure around the country is literally falling apart. The two options for fixing our roads are raising and expanding tolls or raising the federal gasoline tax, which hasn't increased since 1993.

The U.S. Energy Information Administration reports that the federal gas tax is 18.4 cents a gallon, while states average a gas tax of 28.6 cents a gallon. I was surprised to learn taxes aren't a huge chunk of what we pay at the pump. Still, 25 cents a gallon is a lot to add on, but what is the alternative?

I thought about raising tolls where we already have them – in my state on the New Jersey Turnpike and Garden State Parkway – and creating them where they aren't. Then I thought about how the Lincoln Tunnel, which is less than 10 miles from my office and the main artery between New Jersey and Manhattan, already costs $15 per round trip. What are we going to do, raise the toll to $30?

Trucks and taxis use the tunnel multiple times a day. Commuters clog our roads morning, noon and night without a break. On any given morning, the 10-mile ride to Manhattan from my office can easily take 90 minutes or more. Sure, why don't we put toll booths on roads that don't have them because we don't have enough traffic.

Heavy traffic interrupted by tollbooths equals more fuel wasted, which costs drivers more. You waste time sitting in traffic, while goods and services are delivered more slowly. Maybe the multi-state EZ Pass relieves the congestion, but then Big Brother is also watching every mile you drive. Still, we use EZ Pass because there is no other choice if we want to get through the tolls without waiting on growing lines.

So I came to the conclusion that we need the best of two bad solutions – an increase in the gas tax. Doing nothing is not an option, considering the poor shape roads and bridges are in, not only in my area but across the country. And there is some justification in saying since improved infrastructure benefits everyone, everyone driving a vehicle should contribute to making our roads and bridges safer.

Knowing we have to raise gas taxes doesn't mean I have to like it. We're left with this choice because politicians are afraid to make budget cuts, either enough to fund infrastructure spending or smaller cuts combined with a slightly higher tax. There is no compromise in Washington.

My guess? More of the same gridlock. Politicians like giving out the goodies but lack the courage to do what they have to in order to offset spending. Still, even in this environment, a gas tax earmarked exclusively toward infrastructure improvements is some measure of Positive Financial Karma.

A gas tax could lead to a constructive outcome in the form of improved roads, faster commutes and even higher tax revenues (without raising income taxes, no less) because road construction creates new jobs. And it's a heck of a lot better than the alternative – commuter paralysis.

Flat Tax, Fair Tax?

Every election season you hear politicians debating whether to raise or lower taxes. You may have also heard the argument of the flat tax versus fair tax. These two tax approaches may seem like the same thing, but they're not.

For years, the United States has had a progressive tax system, which means the more you make, the more you pay, both in real dollars and as a percentage of taxable income. The higher your income, the higher your tax rate and ultimately the amount of tax you pay.

In a flat tax system, everyone pays the same percentage rate across the board. So if the flat tax is 10 percent, that's what you pay, no matter how much you earn. If, for example, you made $10,000, you pay $1,000 in tax. If you made $1 million, you pay $100,000 in flat tax. Seems like a good idea, right?

The problem with the flat tax is that it will tax many people who do not currently pay any federal income tax.

Wait a minute! You say there are people who don't pay any federal income tax? The Tax Policy Center reports that 44.3 percent, or approximately 76 million people, did not pay any federal income tax in 2016. Granted, 10 percent is a low tax rate, but it's also 10 percent more than nothing that millions of taxpayers now pay under the progressive tax system. The flat tax would potentially be the biggest tax increase of all time, which is why this will not happen, no matter how great the idea.

So why not a fair tax? A fair tax is completely different from a flat tax. Also known as a consumption tax, the fair tax is a type of national sales tax. A lot of the world has something similar, called a value-added tax (VAT) or goods and service tax (GST). The concept is simple enough. The more you consume, the more you pay. This would create a big increase in the price of products we buy and it would shift the collection of taxes to businesses selling goods. But it would be your only federal tax because, ideally, we would first eliminate all other taxes, including income, payroll and other personal and business taxes.

When you have no other taxes to pay, a 10 percent, 20 percent or 30 percent consumption tax seems quite fair, especially if you paid near 40 percent in income taxes before. Interestingly, the Tax Foundation found that such a tax could wipe out more than $3 trillion in national debt in a decade, while adding to the growth of our economy.

A fair tax, however, has a couple of significant built-in obstacles that will ensure we'll never see one. First, it is the opposite of progressive, meaning lower-income taxpayers will pay much more in consumption taxes than they did in income taxes. Second, history is littered with countries that imposed a consumption tax on top of other taxes, not in place of them.

For those reasons and the usual lack of political will, I don't think the United States will replace its progressive income tax system with a fair, or consumption, tax anytime soon.

I believe we'll stay with a progressive tax system, not because it is the best tax system but because it works politically. In other words, politicians don't have to stick their necks out too far by keeping it essentially as is because it allows them to manipulate the tax code to serve their best interests.

Karma? Not so positive if we continue to print dollar bills and borrow from foreign countries to service our debt while our politicians bicker in what seems like a permanent state of self-imposed inertia.

Your alternative in an attempt to achieve Positive Financial Karma when dealing with a mind-numbingly complex tax code? Continue to reduce taxes the best you can – LEGALLY! Even after federal tax changes, there are a number of avenues the Internal Revenue Service allows as ways to reduce your taxes. Ending up in jail for tax evasion is about as negative as it gets when it comes to financial karma.

Don't Mess
With the IRS

Speaking of taxes, the Internal Revenue Code, which regulates how and when you pay taxes, is thousands of pages long. Within this massive collection of rules and regulations, there are many legal methods taxpayers can use to reduce their tax liability.

It would be hard to argue that we wouldn't all be better off if the federal tax code shriveled to the point where we could file our taxes on a postcard. OK . . . maybe accountants like me and tax lawyers might not agree. Anyway, reducing tax complexity is a topic for another time.

This chapter is about what happens when taxpayers try to create their own tax rules, such as declaring personal expenses (including luxury cars and clothing) as business tax deductions. Or what happens when you don't report and pay tax on your income, thus saving 100 percent on taxes – a big no-no.

Let's focus on the real-life example of reality television star Michael "The Situation" Sorrentino, who pleaded guilty in January 2018 to violating federal tax laws. You can't do what The Situation did, no matter how complex your tax returns are or how unfair you believe our collective tax load is.

Sorrentino, who became famous on MTV's "Jersey Shore," and his brother, Marc Sorrentino, allegedly did not report an estimated $9 million of The Situation's income in 2011. Suffice it to say,

The Situation found himself in a very uncomfortable situation when the IRS found out about it.

Hiding income is a cardinal sin when it comes to the IRS. Let me be clear in saying this isn't a gray area, it's black and white. You don't have to be an accountant to know that you need to pay tax on your income. How could anyone think they can make money and not have the government's hand in their pocket? Hence the cliché that the only two certainties in life are death and taxes. My point here is simple: Ignorance is no excuse for not paying your taxes, however unintentional.

The Situation's situation revolved around his alleged intent to intentionally not declare income. And, in this particular case, he had no chance once his accountant rolled over. Gregg Mark, the tax preparer for the Sorrentino brothers, pleaded guilty in 2015 to conspiring to defraud the United States by not including all of Sorrentino's income on the reality star's tax returns.

The IRS is like a shark with blood in the water when it suspects tax fraud. When the IRS determines you did something illegal, the agency will bite down and stay clenched. Despite Congress cutting more than $1 billion from its budget in recent years, the IRS remains an extraordinarily powerful arm of the federal government. If you decide to roll the dice and intentionally hide income, you take a big risk. What's potentially at stake is your freedom. Tax evasion is a felony, which means there is a chance of jail time. Look, we're not talking about forgetting a few hundred dollars earned in miscellaneous income or making honest mistakes on a tax return. This happens occasionally and if the IRS catches these mistakes, taxpayers almost always do no more than pay a penalty along with interest on the amount of untaxed income. After all, no one is perfect and mistakes happen.

A side note: In spite of his IRS troubles, The Situation resumed his reality television career by starring in the MTV sequel, "Jersey Shore: Family Vacation." However, his latest reality show gig didn't stop his sentencing for tax evasion in October 2018. A federal court sentenced Sorrentino to eight months and his brother to two years in jail, where they will face a different reality. The Situation also received two years of supervised release with drug testing and treatment, a $10,000 fine and 500 hours of community service.

The moral of this story? Don't play games with your taxes – do the right thing. No one likes to pay taxes, but you cannot obtain Positive Financial Karma by cheating. Retain a reputable tax professional who knows the tax code and will find all the deductions allowed by the IRS. Trust me, you will sleep a lot better knowing that you had the right intention to create Positive Financial Karma.

Unless you like how you look in stripes.

SALT, No Pepper

I'm reminded of a story I read in The New York Times a while back. A certain billionaire decided to leave New Jersey for the tax-friendly state of Florida, which doesn't have an income tax, bringing with him multiple millions of tax dollars a year New Jersey used to take from him. It will take a lot of everyday taxpayers to make up what this one individual paid, and I don't foresee billionaires lining up to move to New Jersey to maximize how much they pay in state taxes.

I love this state, having spent my entire life here, but New Jersey has become "tax and spend" on steroids. It ranks among the highest of all states in most tax categories, including stratospheric real estate taxes. Is there another way to describe my beloved Garden State? Oh yeah, Bruce Springsteen also lives here.

Yet, droves of people who love New Jersey like me are leaving the state, just as they are fleeing other Northeastern states that, coincidentally or not, impose a significant tax burden on their residents. I concede the point that some people leave for better jobs, follow employers that move out of state and migrate to warmer climates. But you have to add taxes to this list of reasons, too.

Are there really people who think we don't pay enough taxes in New Jersey? The mass exodus to more tax-friendly states would indicate there aren't that many.

New Jersey's tax-and-spend tendencies will thrust it off the financial cliff – possibly before the federal debt does the same to the nation. And then, when businesses and wealthy individuals leave New Jersey in their rear view mirrors, who will we tax? Does anyone in their right mind believe they will stay when they see the (lack of) value for their tax dollar? People may love New Jersey, as I do, but they only stay because they have to. Few people want to stay in an environment where taxes are so punitive.

We get the government we deserve, don't we?

Now taxes are even more punitive in highly taxed states. A feature in the new federal tax law, the State and Local Tax (SALT) provision that limits state income and real estate tax deductions to $10,000 annually, could prove a tipping point in these states. In New York, New Jersey and Connecticut, to name just three states, middle class real estate taxes alone can exceed this limit before you even get around to deducting state and local income taxes.

The impact of the SALT limitation hasn't hit home yet, but I expect high-tax states will see their wealth take off for greener (as in dollars) pastures. SALT creates a perfect storm for states where affordability was already almost nonexistent and tax burdens keep increasing.

This migration of wealth and population from high-tax states will clearly have future political and economic consequences, because the number of representatives a state gets in the U.S. House of Representatives is based on its population. As people migrate to and from states, some states lose representatives while others gain them. As we see in our deeply divided Congress, one vote can make all the difference for major legislation. So state representation matters . . . a lot.

There are a couple of things that can change this exodus of economic and political power. One, Congress could repeal or increase the SALT deduction limit, which is unlikely since the deduction is essentially a tax break low-tax states give their high-tax counterparts. Two, politicians in high-tax states could finally start to trim spending to reduce both debt and tax burdens. I wouldn't count on either right now.

The latter approach, though, could result in Positive Financial Karma for all of us. Failure to cut spending due to a consistently demonstrated lack of political will only results in Positive Financial Karma for the low-tax states that stand as beneficiaries – sort of a karmic transfer.

What can you do? You have a voice. Use it to vote for individual candidates (forget political party) who not only recognize and understand the financial mess, but also exercise fiscal restraint and make difficult and unpopular decisions – like cutting spending. At the same time, you have a voice in determining whether we require term limits for our elected officials.

There's that phrase again – term limits. More on this later.

$15 Minimum Wage

You can spin this any way you like, but minimum wage increases are a tax on employers. And when you increase taxes on businesses, they look for ways to offset or avoid the tax altogether.

I bring this up because politicians across the country are proposing dramatic increases in the minimum wage. The easy part to understand is that the lowest wage earners would benefit, which is a good thing because there are plenty whose families barely get by.

But, as an accountant, I can tell you there is much more than meets the eye on this issue. Because every action has a reaction, a mandated increased wage will have a boomerang effect on the workers it was meant to help, as employers cut hours and jobs in an attempt to limit the additional cost.

An increase in the minimum wage not only increases the direct cost of labor for employers, it also increases their related payroll taxes. But here's something else to think about: Perhaps the costliest aspect would be the cost of raises for those earning more than the minimum wage.

Let's say an employee makes a wage of $7.50 per hour and the entry-level wage increases to $15 per hour. What does the employer do with employees already making $15? Increase them to $30 so that everyone gets the same percentage increase in wages? How many businesses can afford to nearly double the cost of labor and survive? This type of wage compression could be catastrophic to a business.

The $15 minimum wage mandate will, I believe, trigger a number of other events. Not only will businesses soften the blow of a bloated minimum wage by hiring fewer people or reducing their workforce, some will make an investment in technology to replace their workforce. Others may scrap new equipment and technology spending altogether, as their net income is squeezed by higher wages.

It is clear to me that businesses will reduce the number of workers they employ. Is that what government wants? Businesses will also have to pass these additional costs on to the consumer in order to stay solvent, making the products and services we buy more expensive. So, during inflationary periods who gets hurt the most? You guessed it. Minimum wage workers.

The other segment of workers that a $15 minimum wage will undoubtedly negatively affect are high school and college students who look for part-time jobs during the summer or after school. With a higher minimum wage, these jobseekers will have a tougher time finding work as employers balk at paying so much for inexperienced help.

I also believe many companies will abandon or cut back on paid internships because they will simply be too expensive. The programs that do remain will become extremely competitive and many may be left out. This will hurt students who need the money to help pay for school and eliminate the invaluable training that would eventually help lead to full-time jobs.

Proponents argue that a higher minimum wage would mean those workers could buy more and pay more taxes, but I haven't seen any credible evidence to show this yet. Seattle has the oldest law raising the minimum wage to $15 an hour, and first reports have not been kind. The University of Washington studied the issue and found the average low-wage worker lost $125 a month due to a reduction in hours worked related to the higher minimum wage. Another study found that the government-mandated $15 per hour wage in California will cost the state 400,000 jobs by 2023.

Now you might point to announcements by Amazon and other mega-employers that say they will raise their minimum wage to or near $15 per hour and say, "why not?" Here's why not. What looks doable during times of full employment becomes a drag on business when economic rough patches appear. It is doubtful that any but the most profitable businesses can make this commitment to their employees. Time will tell.

The bottom line: minimum wage was not designed to sustain a family, but as a starting point from which employees can raise their income with training and education. Politicians will likely ignore this and motor full steam ahead, riding off the economic cliff with an idea that has bad implications for the economy.

Waiting for the government to mandate your pay raise will do little more than encourage politicians to make a play for your vote. This won't help you advance in your career or create Positive Financial Karma.

My best advice for workers making minimum wage who want to make more money is to work hard, get training and education and take advantage of any and all opportunities to improve your job prospects.

That's creating Positive Financial Karma.

Off With Their Heads!

In Shakespeare's Richard III, the king says, "Off with his head" to a suspected competitor to his throne. This literal separation of head and body would assure the end of this competition.

Fast-forward a few hundred years to Seattle, Washington, where the city not only mandated a minimum wage increase, but also imposed a head tax on its large employers. Originally drawn up as a $500 per head tax on each employee of companies with gross revenues above $20 million annually, the tax was potentially a virtual beheading of company profits for Amazon, Starbucks and other Seattle-based big employers.

Then, with polls showing vast disapproval of the tax from city residents who might have feared the departure of these companies – local economic engines, for sure – the Seattle City Council reversed course and rescinded the tax in 2018. How did we get here from there?

Seattle has a long history of homelessness, and voters initially seemed to favor the head tax as a way to provide affordable housing and other services to address this problem. As is normal practice with most politicians, Seattle's municipal decision-makers opted to tax instead of developing a comprehensive jobs program. Jobs, after all, are the answer to many of these issues. A jobs program would put people back to work and give them the financial means to fend for themselves.

While a jobs program would have been good for society and good for the individuals affected, politicians smelled the estimated $47 million per year the head tax would raise from nearly 600 employers, so they opted for an all-too-familiar approach to the problem. We're talking about government here, and, yes, they did the irresponsible thing – found the nearest individual or company to tax and laid the problem at their feet.

This effort at raising ever-increasing funds from already beleaguered business taxpayers was particularly galling considering its potential effect on jobs. This move was the exact opposite of rewarding companies for creating jobs. So Amazon, Starbucks, other big companies and their employees and residents rose up and began asking what Seattle would do with the head tax revenues. Surprise – there was no plan, just another attempt at taxing and taxing some more.

In the end, polls showed voters had a real fear of these huge employers leaving. Politicians, realizing this reality and fearing for their positions, rescinded the head tax, with the City Council voting 7-to-2 to do so. An Amazon representative recommitted to Seattle and pledged to continue investing in nonprofit organizations that help the homeless. The homeless remained homeless.

Until the next time . . . .

Cents and Centsibility

Financial Anxiety

If government waste is giving you anxiety, take comfort in the fact that there are many things you can control to better your financial situation. I believe almost everyone experiences financial anxiety at one point or another. Trust me: I have been there, too.

Financial anxiety is normal, but how do you overcome it?

Xanax? Prozac?

All kidding aside, you listen to and follow common-sense tips that can help you overcome your financial anxiety and achieve Positive Financial Karma.

Granted, ignoring the noise is difficult. In today's 24/7 social media world, we can't help it. Reports of potential military conflicts blast through the airwaves. We hear about huge stock market swings and listen to political squabbles that border on insanity.

We all hear this noise but financial anxiety, according to a number of surveys, is particularly bad for millennials. That's not surprising. Millennials are the most connected generation and their exposure to information is so much greater than any generation before them.

And everything is so negative.

That's because negative news sells. News editors used to say, "If it bleeds, it leads." And bad financial news is today's figurative bleeding catastrophe.

Don't think I'm putting all the blame on the media. We have all endured the constant barrage of negative news in recent years, but older millennials in particular have faced unprecedented financial challenges during the last decade. They watched as an historic stock market meltdown temporarily destroyed their investments, including those in retirement accounts. At the same time, many struggled under the weight of record college debt. And they found establishing a career difficult to impossible at a time when the economy was shedding jobs.

The perfect storm.

If you're a millennial (or anybody else, for that matter), how do you get beyond these challenges?

Fortunately, finding a good job is easier recently than at any time during the past decade, so look around if you're not happy where you are.

And learn to tune out the noise.

My advice beyond these obvious actions?

Step 1: Get a good education. If you don't have the education needed to reach your career goals, consider going back to school. Take advantage of workplace training and professional education.

If you do not consistently learn and grow in your current job, it's time to move on to a place where you will. Don't waste any more time being stagnant. The world is moving far too fast to be stuck in a routine.

You can do this. How do I know? Because I did. I went back to school twice to obtain advanced degrees while working full time. I didn't do it to build my resume, as I already had my own company by the time I earned each additional diploma. I did it because I simply needed more education to reach my career goals. I did it to learn and apply what I learned. You can, too.

Step 2: Work hard. This is a simple truth that almost always pays dividends over the long term. I believe there is no such thing as luck and nothing is random. Remember karma? It's all about cause and effect. The action of working hard will produce a positive reaction as long as your intention is positive.

And while you're working hard, be sure to stay in the moment. The past is done. The future hasn't happened yet. All you have is the present. That's where you have to live and work.

Step 3: When you feel anxiety coming on, take a deep breath, center yourself and keep your intentions positive.

Step 4: Keep reading. The forthcoming chapters may help you figure your way around life's everyday financial challenges.

Follow these steps and I guarantee that along the way, you will achieve Positive Financial Karma over and over again.

Waste Food,
Want A Lot

Have you ever considered the human and economic cost
of wasting food?

You might think this subject is tongue-in-cheek in a book about
Positive Financial Karma, but it's very serious. Various sources
estimate that Americans waste 30 to 50 percent of our food. The
problem is so prevalent, in fact, that the U.S. Department of Agri-
culture launched its first-ever national food loss and waste goal,
calling for a 50-percent reduction in waste by 2030.

The real numbers behind this call to action are staggering. America
throws out more than 1,250 calories per day per person, or more
than 400 pounds of food per person annually. That's a loss of up to
$218 billion each year, costing a household of four an average of
$1,800 annually. Refuse also has a negative effect on the environ-
ment, wasting an astronomical amount of water and fertilizer.

I grew up trained to never waste food. My parents often said wasting food was a sin. Raised in an Italian family, we had to finish
everything on our plates. This really wasn't too much of a challenge for me because the food was always so good, although it
did create other issues of the "Eat Less, Move More" variety later
in life. But stopping food waste is obviously a challenge to others,
considering the staggering numbers.

How does this happen? For one, we buy food in bulk and buy too much, so some of it lands in the trash can instead of our stomachs. You can reduce food waste by searching for ways to keep bulk food fresh longer, whether you freeze it promptly or refrigerate it properly. I read, for example, that fruits give off natural gases as they ripen, speeding up the spoiling process. Keeping fruit in a bin with only other fruit, it turns out, is one way to slow this process.

By reducing food waste, we achieve a common-cause type of Positive Financial Karma. When we feed more people with food saved from the waste bin, we reduce hunger and save natural resources. There is little that's financially negative about this.

Individually, buying only the food you will eat so nothing is wasted and storing bulk purchases more efficiently can also create Positive Financial Karma. If American families, as the study claims, could save $1,800 per year by not wasting food, imagine the additional Positive Financial Karma this found money could create.

Ask an adviser or go to an online calculator to figure how much contributing $150 monthly —which is $1,800 annually — to a college 529 plan would yield after 15 years.

I'll spare you the trouble: If you earned 6 percent compounded daily, you would accumulate about $43,782 after 15 years. That's not bad for found money, is it?

Or maybe you put the same $150 monthly toward retirement with the same interest rate, but over 30 years. Now that $150 per month turns into $151,463.

That's what I call Positive Financial Karma.

Four Letter Word

Debt.

To some people, debt is a four-letter word. To others, it is the nectar of business success. Debt's relationship to Positive Financial Karma is a function of the type of debt you assume and the reason for it.

If you want to be a successful entrepreneur, you can't be afraid of debt. Real estate investors may spend more time with their lenders than they do looking for properties. Debt is a positive thing if, for example, you borrow money at 5 percent to buy rental property and achieve a 15 to 20 percent return. That's a great return on investment (ROI) and what smart investors try to achieve. Many successful real estate investors have built empires on debt. They became rich using other people's money.

Business owners also take out loans to increase sales, production or a workforce. They strive primarily for a positive ROI, but may get a tax benefit as well. To make debt work, they need to analyze risk, answering "yes" to one big question: Can they pay the loan back when they say they will? Financial institutions don't want bad debt and neither should you if you're a business owner.

For individuals, debt doesn't always provide the same ROI investors get, but it is often necessary. For example, most people can't afford to purchase a home without the help of a loan. Taking on debt is necessary.

I always encourage first-time homebuyers to consider buying a multi-family property – and to live in one unit and rent the others. That way you have rental income each month to offset the mortgage payment. In the end, you build equity and your tenants pay your mortgage (and perhaps your real estate taxes). If you play it right, when you purchase your next home (a single-family) you can hold on to your rental property while it pays for itself and then some.

That's Positive Financial Karma.

That's good debt, but what's bad debt?

Bad debt is a loan of any type with monthly terms you can't afford. Just because a mortgage company offers you a loan with a competitive interest rate doesn't mean you should take it. The Great Recession was littered with the figurative corpses of homeowners whose homes were foreclosed on because they couldn't afford their mortgage payments.

Bad debt is also credit card debt that you don't pay off in full each month. With interest rates of 15 percent and higher, using credit cards in this way is the cardinal sin of money management. When you use credit cards to go on expensive vacations and you dive deeper into the debt hole, you clearly achieve negative financial karma. On top of everything, unsecured credit card debt has no tax benefits for individuals.

If you spend more money than you make, you probably have bad debt. Other types of debt like student loans could be positive or negative, depending on the outcome. You will need to do an analysis to learn if a positive outcome and Positive Financial Karma are in the cards. For example, taking out $100,000 in student loans to become a low-paid museum curator probably is not a wise financial decision. Going $200,000 in debt to become a well-paid plastic surgeon may make more sense.

You also need to compare costs when positive outcomes are similar. If an in-state school is as good as a private university at one quarter of the cost, maybe you or your student stays in state.

Most state schools are just as good, if not better, than many private universities and provide a much better ROI on your education dollars. A diligent student intent on obtaining marketable skills can do so nearly anywhere. Then again, schools like Harvard are clearly great "employment agencies," which is what most top schools are. Therefore, the additional dollars paid for an elite school can also provide an exceptional ROI.

To summarize, when it comes to college "go state or go great."

Consider these and other factors and make the right choice for the right reasons to achieve Positive Financial Karma.

A few other ways to move away from negative financial karma toward a good outcome with positive intent:

- If you have credit card balances, consider paying a little more each month to the card with the highest rate until it is paid off;

- If your new car loan payments are ending soon, consider keeping the car loan-free and use the payments
  to pay down bad debt;

- If you have a 30-year mortgage, make one extra payment a year and cut seven to eight years off your term
  (if you don't have a prepayment penalty);

- If you're looking for a mortgage, compare the much
  lower total costs of a 15-year mortgage versus a
  30-year mortgage. You can save tens or hundreds of
  thousands of dollars over the life of the mortgage for
  only a few hundred extra dollars a month.

Credit Scores

If you are planning to buy a new home, one of the most important steps you can take is to build and maintain a good credit score. Even if you think you have great credit, mistakes on your credit reports can lower your credit scores and potentially make getting a mortgage very expensive or impossible.

It's vital to find out your score and raise it, if necessary. Start by getting your reports from the three major credit reporting agencies: Equifax, TransUnion and Experian. Federal law entitles you to receive a free credit report once a year from each agency and anytime you are turned down for credit for any reason. Get your reports at www.AnnualCreditReport.com. You will need to provide your name, address, Social Security number and date of birth to verify your identity.

If you find mistakes on any report, put the discrepancies in writing and notify the agency involved. Typically, the agency will have 30 days to investigate your claim, after which it must report to you the findings, report the results to the other two major agencies and provide you with a free credit report that won't count toward your free annual report. If you aren't satisfied, you may dispute the findings in writing, which will go on your report. Either way, you can ask the credit reporting company to send correction notices to anyone who received your report in the past six months, or in the previous two years in the case of employment credit inquiries.

Once you have your credit reports settled, you might get your credit score for a fee from credit score pioneer www.myfico.com or for free through an increasing number of credit cards. Learn what incurs a fee and what you can get for free and monitor your score.

Cultivating a high credit score is a big deal, not only for the best interest rates on loans but for car insurance rates and employment opportunities. Even a difference of 10 points can be a big deal. And a difference of one percentage point in interest – that's 1 percent -- is staggering when you're talking about a $250,000 mortgage over 30 years.

At 4 percent, you'll pay about $1,194 per month and $430,000 over the life of the mortgage. At 5 percent the monthly nut becomes $1,342 while the total balloons to just over $484,000, a difference of $54,000 over the life of the loan. Which begs the question: How do you raise your credit score? After all, 650 may be adequate but 750 and higher is where the most favorable interest rates reside.

To start improving your score, make a budget with the intent to pay down your highest credit card balances. Next, pay off as much other debt as possible, but don't cancel your cards. Banks look at your debt-to-available-credit ratio and the lower the ratio the better. Ultimately, just stop buying stuff and work to lower your debt load to make yourself an ideal candidate for the best interest rates. Then, Positive Financial Karma is sure to follow.

If you can't figure this out on your own, seek out a nonprofit org-anization that can help. Credit counseling won't hurt your credit score, but debt management – which includes reworked payments – may. The Federal Trade Commission (FTC) offers some tips on finding legitimate credit counseling at www.consumer.ftc.gov/articles/0153-choosing-credit-counselor.

Focusing on responsible financial behavior can ultimately lead to a better credit score and create Positive Financial Karma.

The Exploding
Cost of College

Let's face it. Parents would love to send their kids to the most expensive schools if they could afford it, but this is becoming increasingly problematic. The cost for tuition, room and board and fees at top private universities is between $40,000 and $75,000 annually. State colleges, once a haven for those fleeing high education costs, are also becoming prohibitively expensive. As a result, the number of parents who can pay for college without borrowing or other financial assistance is shrinking.

And the jury is still out on a workable "free" college solution, meaning many parents will still experience sleepless nights as they figure out how to pay for their children's college costs.

In this environment, it is crucial to come up with a game plan. Learn how to calculate the return on your college investment. In my opinion, the best strategy is: "Go state or go great." Even with some big-name state schools costing an arm and a leg for out-of-state students, in-state students typically find much lower costs. If you want lower costs still, consider community college as a pit stop for gaining required coursework credit. Trust me, the difference in the quality of the education is not substantial.

You might even urge Junior to explore the possibility of learning a trade. Plumbers, electricians and other tradespeople often earn a higher income than college graduates with humanities' degrees

– without most of the cost. They may even have an easier time becoming business owners than others do. That's Positive Financial Karma.

Higher education – like most anything else in life – is not free and never will be. You can argue that it is human nature to appreciate your education when you have a financial stake in it.

Kids need skin in the game. When you spend money to accomplish anything, you'll care a whole lot more about it. This is also Positive Financial Karma.

Attention students: If you're ready to attend college or about to, I'd like you to pay particular attention to this sentence:

Mom and Dad should not pay for your college education at the expense of their retirement readiness!

The Urban Institute recently reviewed statistics from the U.S. Department of Education and found that 17 of every 100 Americans who owe money on federal student loans are over age 50. This age group owed $247 billion in federal student debt, three times the amount owed in 2003, accounting for inflation.

Parents naturally want what's best for their kids, but this desire to give their children the best can hurt them later on. So why not consider ways to lower the costs for all involved. Go state. Take a few gap years to work and save money before attending college.

Get community college and advanced placement credits. Check out work/study programs to gain experience and further defray costs.

And by all means, please don't dump this responsibility on your parents. We know you love each other. But they probably don't want to live with you when they retire, and you probably share their sentiments.

Is Grad School
Worth It?

Americans owed $1.53 trillion in student loans during the second quarter of 2018, according to the Federal Reserve. Is it worth it?

While this number is staggering, the growth in only 12 years is equally stunning. In the second quarter of 2006, Americans owed $487 billion, more than three times less than what they owe today.

All of these numbers convince me – and should convince you – that you need to calculate your ROI when deciding whether a graduate degree is worth it. This is no different from the approach you would take before deciding on any other investment – and, make no mistake about it, your education is an investment.

You can start by making certain assumptions. People in finance, engineering and some sciences tend to benefit the most from earning a graduate degree.

Then get specific.

How much will your degree cost and how much extra can you expect to earn over your lifetime? You need both parts of this equation to come up with an accurate answer. For example, a museum curator earning a graduate degree at an inexpensive state school without a commensurate increase in compensation may not make financial sense. A Wall Street worker earning an MBA from the most expensive Ivy League school may actually make more economic sense, considering the substantial increase in pay and added heft to a resume.

When doing your ROI calculations, remember to include the total cost of any loans you need to take for your advanced degree. For example, if you have a 10-year, $50,000 student loan at 6 percent, your actual cost over the life of the loan will be more than $66,000 if you don't pay it off early. How much more could this $66,000 investment generate in future earnings? This is the question you must answer.

Before springing for that loan, consider other ways to pay for graduate school. Your field of graduate study may offer merit scholarships for academic or work achievements. Your employer may offer interest-free school loans or reimburse you for a portion of your education costs. In either situation, you need to consider how you will balance what is probably full-time work with graduate school study. And, increasingly, bigger employers are now offering a student loan repayment benefit, which I urge you to explore if available.

As with any other investment you make in your lifetime, conducting a comprehensive ROI calculation will help you take the actions that can lead to Positive Financial Karma.

Equal Work, Equal Pay

Equal pay was in the news in the United Kingdom for a good portion of last year after all companies with at least 250 employees
were required to report pay data by gender. Pay transparency, in
which companies are required to publicly disclose pay for male
and female workers, may actually work to close the gender pay
gap across the pond and in the United States.

The first pay transparency reports in 2018 caused major outrage
in the United Kingdom. About eight in 10 companies paid women
less than men for the same work. It goes without saying that there
shouldn't be a gender gap in pay. Equal jobs done equally well
should mean equal pay. If this report shows anything, it's that pay
inequities exist worldwide, not just in the United States, where
women are gaining slowly but still earn only 81 percent of what
men earn.

In this country, we continue to struggle over the right response. In
2016, President Obama proposed to remedy the inequity by requir-
ing companies with at least 100 workers to report similar pay data
by sex, age and job to the Equal Employment Opportunity Commission. In 2018, President Trump killed the initiative, saying it would
create too big a financial and time burden on businesses.

I'm generally skeptical about any government approach to a problem. Companies have enough regulations to follow and paperwork
to process, and it generally never works out when our politicians
try to regulate behavior. However, I couldn't agree more that

equal performance should result in equal pay. And I understand that many women start out behind the eight ball with careers delayed or interrupted as they start and care for families. If you believe free market economics demand that compensation reflects contributions to an organization, there shouldn't be a gender pay gap, hiatus from work or not. Unfortunately, while we make small gains, the gap remains.

How do you fix the problem? If you are a business owner, strive for fairness because this is what equal pay for equal performance comes down to – fairness. Make merit matter. If you are an employee who believes that you contribute more to your company than a higher-paid male doing the same job, either ask your company to make you financially equal or discreetly find another firm that will.

While we may do better than other countries, we can do much better. As the spotlight continues to shine on this subject, I believe we will eventually reach a point where we achieve equal compensation for everyone. When companies reward performance without regard for gender, they motivate and incentivize employees to perform at a higher level.

More productive employees mean more profitable companies and — you guessed it – Positive Financial Karma.

When Emotions Lead, Checkbooks Bleed

For the past century, owning a home has been the American dream – or at least some real estate companies would have us think so. They have led us to believe that home ownership is a win-win proposition because real estate prices always increase, right?

Wrong!

In the aftermath of the Great Recession, real estate prices indeed fell. After 2008, countless Americans found they couldn't afford the loans that banks and mortgage firms had sold them. They forfeited their homes, owing more than the homes were worth and wrecking their credit ratings in the process.

Today, the combination of the memory of this severe economic downturn, just when millennials were starting out in the work force, and their record student debt has made them less likely to own homes than previous generations at the same age.

This is a good spot to tell you that not all homes are bad investments. Rental properties could be great investments. But, if truth be told, owning a home for personal use is not such a great investment. When you factor in mortgage costs, real estate taxes, interest, insurance and maintenance – the total costs of home ownership – ultimately, it is about money going out the door.

Just look at the cost of home ownership over time, starting with points you pay to acquire a mortgage and the interest paid throughout the course of the mortgage. If you buy a home for $200,000 and keep the mortgage for 30 years, your total costs could exceed $400,000! You would be hard-pressed to find a home whose return on investment is positive after running these numbers.

You could argue that your ROI will skyrocket because your home is in a prime location. I made that argument to myself with a house on the bay at the Jersey shore. It was a great investment until Superstorm Sandy blew through and the bay wound up in my house. My point is this: Great locations change.

I would argue you're better off buying investment property and renting a place to live in, but I also know that buying your "dream house" is in large part emotion mixed with a little logic. Emotion and money never mix well. I'm not saying you shouldn't buy a home, but I do caution you to understand your decision and its financial costs. Know that owning may cost you more than renting both in the short term and over time.

If you're thinking about buying a home in the near future, I would suggest you ask yourself some tough questions and run the numbers.

Can you afford the home?

Qualifying for a mortgage doesn't mean you can afford it. You know how much money you spend per month and what's left over. Do you really have enough extra income for a first-time or a bigger mortgage? You may if you live in a high-rent area like New York

City or San Francisco and its suburbs, where home ownership costs may (or may not) be comparable to renting. The choice is clearer in many other regions, where rents are significantly lower than mortgage costs and real estate taxes.

Do you understand the impact of interest rates?

A $300,000, 30-year fixed mortgage at 5 percent would cost you $1,610 per month (not counting home insurance, mortgage insurance, closing costs, home repairs and real estate taxes) totaling almost $580,000 over 30 years. Bump the interest up to 6 percent and you'll pay $1,799 monthly and $647,515 total. That's almost a $70,000 difference over the life of the mortgage. And keep in mind that we are still seeing historically low interest rates, despite recent increases. In fact, mortgage rates were double or higher three decades ago than they are today.

Will you live in this home for a few years?

Even if your home appreciates modestly, you need three to five years to recoup closing costs and real estate fees. Realize it is also easier getting out of a rental than getting out from under a mortgage should you need to move quickly.

Have you factored in peripheral costs?

Before making the biggest purchase of your life, find out how much replacing an electric service or heating system costs. See how high the costs of a new roof or other structural repairs are in your area. Don't forget to factor in things like increased travel costs if you move farther away from work where home prices are less expensive. Also, don't forget to include your other debt – existing debt like student loans and future debt like a child's education.

If you do all the research, understand how the numbers work and still want to own your personal residence, more power to you. Just understand that the bill comes due regularly for the next 30 years. Whatever your choice, you'll get a measure of Positive Financial Karma if you do your homework to make sure the decision is right for you.

A Bad Investment

If you plan to buy a vehicle that isn't a classic, you will make a bad investment – plain and simple. Previously I talked about how buying a home isn't a guaranteed moneymaker. Buying a car, on the other hand, is an absolute money-shredder.

Imagine buying a home for a few hundred thousand dollars and then watching it bleed value little by little until it becomes practically worthless. That's what happens when you buy a new car at an average of almost $36,000, or a used car at an average of $20,000, only to watch it bleed value even more quickly.

This is the definition of "crazy," right? That's the epitome of negative return on investment and the definition of negative financial karma.

In my mind, buying a new car or SUV is the worst investment you can make. Even a good investment in a car that will become a classic isn't immediately positive because the value virtually disappears until it hits its magical birthday at 25 years, assuming the car is in peak shape.

As with buying a home, deciding how to spend your transportation dollars is an emotional decision. I recommend you take all the emotion out of your decision and evaluate your alternatives.

First, look at the total cost of buying a car: It can include insurance, repairs, extended warranties, satellite radio, your down payment and monthly payments – with interest. Finance $30,000 at 5 percent and you'll pay $34,787 after six years in principal and interest. Not a lot of Positive Financial Karma here.

Next, look at the alternatives. You could lease instead of buy, but you would still be responsible for maintenance, repairs and fuel, plus you could incur additional expense if you exceed mileage allowances or bring the vehicle back in less-than-perfect condition. The problem with this approach is that car dealers have you on the hook when the lease expires. "Why not lease a brand-new car," they'll say, "at little more than you're paying now?" Human nature says you'll likely accept the deal and recommit to a continuous stream of costly monthly lease payments.

Another alternative could be to keep your old warhorse as long as repairs don't cost you a fortune because you are, after all, free and clear of car payments.

And one more option could be to use a ride-sharing service, a recent phenomenon that has reduced the cost of getting from here to there in major metropolitan areas. While it is debatable whether working for one of these companies is a good deal, they are driving down the transportation cost for people who use them – a simple example of supply and demand.

Public transportation and walking are other cost-effective alternatives, but you'll have to consider your convenience and time – especially if you think your time is worth something.

Certainly these two options and ride-sharing or car services are better investments than infinite monthly car payments.

Whether you live in a rural area or a city, evaluate all of your options to determine your best investment. Compare alternative transportation costs to those of owning or leasing, plus the accompanying tolls, fuel and repairs. Look at your wallet, your budget and your travel needs to come up with the solution that gives you the best shot at Positive Financial Karma.

Buy a Used Car

Sometimes you have no transportation alternatives other than your own vehicle. If you live in a region where this is your only option, consider buying a used car instead of a new one. Here's why:

The moment you drive a new car off the lot, it loses value. Some estimates show a new car loses 15 to 25 percent per year and up to 60 percent in the first five years. That's a heck of a bad investment, if you ask me.

If you really need a vehicle, your best option could be a used car, and there has never been a better time to buy one. The volume of leased cars in the U.S. market right now is at an all-time high. Americans lease nearly one-third of all new cars in the U.S., returning them when their leases expire in two to four years and creating a huge inventory of used cars.

This is where supply and demand meet again. A huge glut of relatively new, formerly leased vehicles fills the secondary market, driving down cost and presenting buyers with a wide choice of quality used cars at a fraction of new car prices.

When you strip the emotion from your buying decision, a vehicle gets you from point A to point B. Luxury aside, there are a few ways to buy a used car economically and the current market is perfect for buying one. Do your due diligence and you can get a great buy.

Start by setting a price range, not a ballpark estimate of what you will spend, and don't exceed this amount. Check vehicle history reports via a 17-digit Vehicle Identification Number (VIN). Some companies, including CARFAX and AutoCheck, charge for this service, while others, including www.vehiclehistory.com, provide reports for free.

While you shop, realize some cars were repaired after major wrecks. Others were declared total losses by their insurers due to fire, flood or accident, in which case you'll know because the vehicle will have what's known as a salvage title.

Speaking of titles, make sure your potential used car's title is free and clear of liens and loans. Check out the reliability of the models you like from trusted sources like Consumer Reports. Negotiate your best price by checking prices via Kelley Blue Book and Edmunds for the same vehicles with the same features.

Do your homework and you can make a smart purchase that will serve your needs at a good price. Someone needs to sell a car and you need to buy a car. Buying the right used car for the right price is a winning situation for everyone involved and another step in your quest to achieve total Positive Financial Karma.

Cryptocurrency

When credit cards first came into existence, many people questioned whether they would ever be widely used. Turns out they had no problem gaining acceptance, so it's easy to see how some people believe that cryptocurrency will become an accepted way to pay for anything. Skeptics are many, though, and the jury is out on whether cryptocurrency will ever gain the acceptance credit cards have.

While you may not be familiar with cryptocurrency, you probably have heard of bitcoin, the most widely used of all the alternative currencies. Bitcoin, like all cryptocurrency, is a decentralized digital currency you buy with your traditional currency – cash. Think of bitcoin as you would a stock, except you can use bitcoin as legal tender. You might buy a share of XYZ Corporation for $30. Now if you could use this share as cash, it wouldn't maintain the same value because stock prices fluctuate. So does the value of bitcoin.

Supply and demand come into play here, just as it does with the stock market. If bitcoin is in high demand, prices go up – as high as almost $20,000 per unit near the end of 2017. If demand falls, prices follow – bitcoin rose from under $1,000 per unit in early 2017, to the aforementioned high, and then fell to under $6,500 per unit within 10 months. With prices this volatile, some bitcoin investors suffered big losses – just as you can by investing in stocks.

I'm not going to get into a complicated description of where to buy and sell bitcoin, but I will tell you how it burst onto the scene.

A fellow from Japan supposedly invented the concept in 2008. Some financial consumers, scarred by the last global financial meltdown and the roiled banking system, showed interest in this new way to bypass the banks – the middle men – and cryptocurrency transformed from an idea into a fledgling currency.

Theoretically, bitcoin and others like it can work. With no central force behind it, cryptocurrency is conceptually incorruptible. Transactions happen strictly online going from person to person. Realize, though, that bitcoin is only as secure as your computer or smartphone, which will store your currency. If you invest in bitcoin, you must have up-to-date security and backup software to keep your investment safe.

Transactions are also anonymous, which is positive because Big Brother can't snoop into your business and negative if and when someone uses the currency for illegal purposes. However, adoption of the new currency is still slow, just as credit card acceptance was gradual in the beginning.

Is bitcoin real or will it become a fad?

My clients and students ask me this question all the time. While currencies like the dollar, the euro and others around the world are real, they remain only as good as the government backing them. In some countries, corruption killed the value of the currencies tied to the full faith and strength of their nations.

Bitcoin, on the other hand, is tied to nothing — decentralization is a major selling point of this newer currency. So while it isn't mainstream yet, I believe cryptocurrency is here to stay and will become the way the financial world turns in our lifetimes. You can already find bitcoin in IRAs and some mutual funds.

Should you be an early adopter? Anyone seriously considering making an investment in cryptocurrency should do their home-work, understand how it works and know where to use it to make this alternative currency a contributor to your Positive Financial Karma.

Clean Up Your Finances

When your car is dirty, you wash it. When your yard is cluttered, you clear it up. When the kids drop toys all over the house, you put the toys – or the kids – away. You do these chores regularly; otherwise, the mounds of dirt, clutter and toys would become unmanageable.

Ever wonder why you don't do the same with your finances?

I understand the reluctance to clean up – or review – your finances. Financial and insurance types are famous for spewing hard-to-understand phrases and concepts. It gets to the point where your eyes glaze over and you just want to put any thought of a financial review to the side. There's always tomorrow, right?

Wrong.

Life changes, and life goes on whether you adapt to this change or not. In order to create and maintain Positive Financial Karma, you need to review your financial situation at least once a year, or more frequently when warranted.

I know the task can seem daunting, but you can conduct an annual review with little pain when you work with financial professionals who speak to you in terms you understand and who answer your questions.

To make it easier, consider breaking down your finances into different areas: Personal finance, education planning, retirement planning, risk management of your assets, insurance planning and estate planning. If you own a business, create a separate section for that, too. Breaking down each area of your financial life into manageable bits can make a financial review less imposing. So let's start by looking at each area, one by one.

Personal Finance

Your personal finance housekeeping includes budgeting for everyday expenses, saving for a car or home, and starting or maintaining an emergency fund. If you are working toward buying a car or home, you'll find places in your budget where you can cut expenditures and put additional money toward big financial goals. An emergency fund equal to three to nine months of income is also important should unemployment, sickness or another event temporarily stop your income stream.

Education Planning

I talk a lot about how to cut education costs in this book because it is such a big financial goal. Start by putting away a little at a time as soon as possible to build a college funding kitty. Coverdell Education Savings Accounts (ESAs) let you put a little away each year and take tax-free withdrawals for qualified education expenses. A 529 plan – each state has one – lets you put more money away and also offers tax advantages, while giving the person funding it more flexibility on the use of its funds.
One caution: You'll want to invest in relatively safe investments as your child or grandchild nears college age.

Retirement Planning

It's never been more important to plan for a financially comfortable retirement. More companies and even governments are putting the onus for saving on their employees via 401(k), 403(b) and 457 plans, as opposed to guaranteed defined benefit pensions, which are disappearing from the workplace. These savings plans, which you have to manage for the long term, require the same approach as saving for education expenses or a home does. You can invest more aggressively when you are far from your goal, but safety of principal is best as you near the goal.

Many people make the mistake of putting off saving for retirement for later, but, in this case, the early bird gets the worm. If you are age 27 and put $500 per month into a 401(k) for 40 years earning 7 percent compounded monthly, you'll have more than $1.3 million for retirement. If you think you can start at age 47 and double your monthly deposit to equal the same amount, you'll be surprised to learn you can't. After 20 years, a $1,000 monthly contribution earning 7 percent compounded monthly will only total around $521,000. Clearly, time matters, so it's important to contribute something toward retirement as early as possible.

Risk Management

You might also call this section investment planning, and it's important that you do it right. When you're young, you can be more aggressive with stocks or mutual funds because you'll have time on your side to smooth out any volatility. When you near a goal, however, you'll want to be careful where you put your money. Investment planning involves how you allocate your assets – or, in English, the percentage of funds you direct to varied investments as part of your overall portfolio.

Start with an investment strategy, which you should review every 6 to 12 months. Follow the strategy, which should serve your purposes in good times and bad, if it is well-planned and you consider your financial goals, risk tolerance and time horizon. Work with an investment professional if you have a complicated investment strategy, or perhaps do it yourself through online trading sites or robo-advisers for less complicated investing needs.

Insurance Planning

You'll have different needs at various times in your life, so you'll want to review these needs and your insurance coverage periodically, especially after changes including births, deaths and divorce. Start with health insurance – you can't do without it because health care is expensive. Later in life you'll need to transition to Medicare, which is actually multiple health insurance policies that separately cover hospital stays, doctor visits, prescription drugs and even deductibles.

Life insurance and disability income insurance are also important – the former takes care of your beneficiaries (your loved ones) financially should the unthinkable happen, while the latter protects your ability to earn a living. Consider long-term care insurance with the help of an adviser as you reach age 55 or so, when rates are usually their least expensive, or put funds aside for this purpose in another financial vehicle.

Explore your employee benefit options to buy at least a base of insurance coverage at low group insurance costs. Don't forget you'll need home or renter's insurance and liability insurance. If you live in certain regions of the country, you may also need additional insurance to protect against windstorm, flood or earthquake damage. If you have expensive jewelry, art or other collectibles, you will need specialized coverage to financially protect yourself against loss or damage.

Estate Planning

If you think estate planning is only for the wealthy, you would be wrong. Although new federal tax laws substantially increased the threshold at which the IRS begins taxing your estate after your death, some small-business owners' estates may still exceed that amount. Not only that, but many states still assess their own estate and inheritance taxes at much lower thresholds.

Estate planning is important not only to shield assets from taxes for your heirs, but also for you while you're on this Earth. If you don't have a will, financial and health care powers of attorney and an advanced health care directive, you should consult an attorney to create them.

These sections barely scratch the surface of things you'll need to consider to keep your financial house in order to maintain Positive Financial Karma. I can write books about each area of your financial life – and I may – but at least you can use these few words as thought-starters to learn more.

Whatever you do, review your finances. Life will change, and it's important your finances keep pace.

Overcoming Financial Trouble in Retirement

If you're nearing or in retirement and you're in debt, join the crowd. According to the Employee Benefit Research Institute, better than two of three families with heads aged 55 or older had debt. That's up from 53.8 percent in 1992. And, disturbingly, the number of households with a head 75 or older saw their debt increase by nearly 60 percent, the fastest growth increase.

This is a very serious issue. The goal of most any retiree should be debt-free living in retirement: This means no mortgage, no car payment, no credit card bills. Yet, I see more people loading up on debt before retirement.

One major contributor to the debt load of retirees is a child's or grandchild's college expenses. Some of my clients nearing retirement are actually still paying off loans for private primary and secondary education for their kids. Others took out home equity loans and retirement plan loans to pay for their kids' education, a bad recipe for retirement.

The time to get out of this debt black hole is well before you retire, which means you need to start planning for your retirement yesterday, not when you reach age 64. Gain a measure of Positive Financial Karma by first paying down your debt with the highest interest rates. If you can earn more by investing than the 15 to 20 percent some people pay in credit card interest, please tell me who your investment adviser is.

If you make a dent in your debt and find you still owe too much near age 65 or beyond, there are a few ways out of this hole. First, map out your income and expenses and eliminate purchases you don't need, putting this found money toward your debt. If you can still work, do so to speed the process along.

If you can't work, you might consult a legitimate credit counseling service to see if you can get creditors to agree on more favorable credit terms or lower payments. You may even be able to negotiate dollars off your bill, as is sometimes the case with hospital bills. Credit counseling shouldn't affect your credit score negatively, but negotiating down your total debt will.

If you need to do more, consider downsizing your home and selling belongings with value. Don't forget to look at the cash value of any life insurance policy you own and, as a last resort, reverse mortgages as two other potential aides to your debt-paying efforts. If you live in a high-tax state, you may even consider moving.

Do the best you can and figure out a way to live within your means, eliminate your debt and look to the future. Don't worry about the past because you can't change it. With the right intent and subsequent action, you can turn negative financial karma into a positive future.

Death and Taxes

You probably have heard this paraphrased old saying attributed to Benjamin Franklin: "The only certainties in life are death and taxes." In some cases, it's also certain your family will pay death taxes on your assets after you die.

Also known as estate and inheritance taxes, death taxes are essentially a way for the government to get a second bite of the apple. The first bite is taken when the taxpayer is alive and earns income, and the second is on the assets accumulated up to the time of the taxpayer's death. As of this writing, the nonprofit Tax Foundation notes that 12 states and the District of Columbia impose an estate tax, while six levy an inheritance tax.

At least one state, Maryland, wins the grand prize by taxing estates of dead people both ways. So don't die as a resident of Maryland!

Of the two, estate taxes are typically far more expensive. The federal government, which has its own estate tax, used to be far more invasive at the turn of the century, when taxes began on estates starting at only $675,000 and the top tax rate was 55 percent. Geez, this wouldn't buy you a bungalow in some California locations.

Today's federal estate tax exemption – the amount of assets in an estate that escapes this particular death tax – was more than $11 million per person in 2018 and the top tax rate is 40 percent. Still, the higher threshold doesn't mask the fact that any death tax is a way to tax you twice – first on what you earned and then on the same assets your estate passes on to beneficiaries.

Despite the inherent unfairness of estate taxes, don't expect much more change than we've seen in recent years, when some states eliminated their estate taxes. In fact, I wouldn't put it past cash-starved states to reinstate death taxes. How will taxpayers react? I expect we will see a repeat of a time when some people left these states to establish residences in other states without estate taxes. You would be surprised how much strategic planning goes into relocating in order to avoid paying taxes, even after death. Taxing the rich always plays well among the voting masses, but I always say that wealth is mobile. So the wealthy will move as a tax play.

Estate taxes are as old as the Roman Empire, but the modern estate tax in the United States wasn't born until the early 1900's. At the time, a few super-rich families – names like Morgan, Carn-egie and Rockefeller – controlled almost all of the wealth in this country. With no other way to extract money from these families, Congress created the estate tax.

Over time, the government lowered the threshold on who and what qualified for the estate tax, while simultaneously raising the tax rates. Whereas the government once initiated this tax in an attempt to break up family dynasties, over time they collected death taxes from average people who had to sell family homes and businesses to pay Uncle Sam.

Today, even with a higher asset threshold, I don't believe any amount of death taxes creates Positive Financial Karma –

especially for families who are beneficiaries of these estates. It doesn't seem right that people who worked hard to achieve financial success should have their heirs pay taxes a second time on hard-earned assets. This is punishment for financial accomplishment.

Who doesn't want to be financially successful? This is encouraged in a capitalist society. Why should government have the power to redirect your post-mortem financial intentions by double-taxing? How does the government know better?

Look, if you want to give your money away before or at the time of your death, you can do it on your own. Two of the richest people in the world right now, Warren Buffet and Bill Gates, are giving vast amounts of money – most of their wealth – to charity. They are creating positive intentions so that wherever those dollars go, they should have Positive Financial Karma behind them.

Can you say politicians have that same intention, that same karma? If you believe your wealth can benefit the government and believe politicians can distribute your tax money appropriately, by all means keep it unprotected and let the tax collectors take it when you're gone. And if you believe in contributing your wealth for the benefit of the greater good, by all means take the steps to make that happen today and spread your Positive Financial Karma around.

Estate Planning

One of the most proactive things adults of any age can do is to plan for the disposition of their estates. You don't have to be rich to need to plan. That's why everyone should have a will, which is the foundation of any estate plan.

Death is never a pleasant thought. After all, who wants to think about dying? From time to time, I come across people who have convinced themselves that creating a will can cause their death. As odd as this may sound, it's more common than you'd think. It often takes quite a bit of persuasion on my part to assure them otherwise. Physical death is an absolute and recognizing this reality is the first step. So it's part of my job to have clients accept that they are going to die at some point, they can't predict when and they need to properly plan for it.

Here's the thing about beginning your estate planning process: If you don't plan, the government will do it for you. In other words, everybody has an estate plan – either it's their own or it's their state's laws that will dictate who gets what assets. Incredibly, there have been rich and famous people such as Howard Hughes and Prince who never made a last will and testament. As a result, long legal battles ensued to sort out the details. The Hughes estate, for example, took decades to settle. Without a will, the courts ultimately decided who got all of his "stuff."

While your stuff may not be as considerable or valuable, you still want to make these decisions for yourself before you die. Obviously, it's too late after that.

Start with a will to name guardians and make arrangements for the upbringing of minor children and special-needs adult children. In the latter case, you'll want to work with advisers to choose guardians you absolutely trust and to create a financial plan to provide for your children throughout their lives.

While you are young and healthy is a great time to start composing this planning document, which you may change multiple times as circumstances in your life change. As part of this introductory process, create legal and health care powers of attorney, in which you appoint someone to make decisions for you in these areas if you can't because of incapacitation. Also consider writing out an advanced directive that outlines which life-saving health care treatments you may or may not want.

If you don't want the public to read the details about how your assets are distributed after death, you might also consider a living trust. Small-business owners who don't want competitors poking their noses in their business and wealthy families that want to avoid the public spotlight often put their assets into a trust, where distribution of assets remains private.

Wealthy individuals might prefer to use special types of trusts, in which decisions are typically irrevocable, to shield their assets from tax authorities as they pass to family and charities. While federal estate taxes don't kick in until reaching a higher limit than before, states can and will tax assets at much, much lower thresholds. Putting assets into an irrevocable trust can protect them.

All of this planning constitutes a series of positive intentions that will create Positive Financial Karma for multiple people and organizations long after you're gone. Whether your only concern is passing a sentimental piece of costume jewelry to a grandchild or you need to protect considerable wealth from taxes, start planning early and review regularly.

When Politicians Strike

Political Gerrymandering

In 2018 the Supreme Court more or less punted on two cases of gerrymandering, leaving two questionable voting districts intact before the midterm elections. In my mind, gerrymandering – redrawing voting districts for partisan purposes – is one of the many reasons I believe we need term limits for our elected officials.

Gerrymandering is the ultimate display in political corruption. Consider these districts in question: One was drawn up by Republicans in Wisconsin and the other by Democrats in Maryland. These and other states, notably Texas and Pennsylvania, have districts that look like wall splatter, a ridiculous, deliberate manipulation of boundaries for political gain designed to keep parties in or out of office.

No one is innocent. Both parties complain about this practice but all too willingly participate in it. When politicians gerrymander districts, the issue becomes whether the newly redrawn districts have fair representation for all voters. Fair representation in mapping should be the goal, but we all know politicians will do most anything for political gain. Nothing else matters but winning re-election, and these crazy districts are drawn up to protect politicians and their parties.

I'm disappointed the Supreme Court didn't stop this practice in 2018, but there will be other cases like this in the future. Meanwhile, get ready for a new dose of gerrymandering, as the states redraw districts in 2020 after the 10-year census is completed.

Before then, term limits anyone? If politicians can't control their worst impulses, it is imperative that like-minded voters band together to demand term limits. Your Positive Financial Karma depends on it.

Race and College Admissions

As you must know by now, I have strong opinions about how to pay for life's expenses, including higher education costs. I am baffled, however, about how to answer the continuing question of whether race, religion or gender should play any role in college admissions.

The Trump administration reminded us of this issue in the summer of 2018 when it reversed guidelines that urged colleges and universities to consider diversity when making decisions about admissions. A few months later, the Supreme Court heard a case brought by Students for Fair Admissions, which alleged Harvard University violated their civil rights by limiting admissions of Asian-American students due to diversity guidelines that favored less qualified applicants of other ethnicities.

This is a tough subject filled with lots of emotion and great points on all sides. I believe we should celebrate and promote diversity. But should we follow a discriminatory policy against certain groups whose members are bypassed for admission by less qualified applicants in the name of diversity?

I truly struggle to find an answer to this question, because it seems that whatever answer you choose, one group or another will feel slighted. What if admission policies were blind to race? What if they were completely anonymous? Would this result in limiting representation of some ethnic groups?

I'm not sure we can achieve diversity in higher education without discriminating. What is fair for one group may be unfair to another, and maybe race-blind admissions are not the best thing for society. I understand that the intent of race-based admissions is good, but there are always unintended consequences. At the same time, basic instinct tells me that discrimination is wrong and disrupts the natural order of things.

I can't for the life of me provide you with a concrete solution. But if I had to make a choice, I would choose a blind admissions process because it would be the fairest.

Personal Responsibility
Creates Job Security

I'm writing this as news of this summer's biggest primary election shocker shakes the political establishment. Self-described Democratic Socialist Alexandria Ocasio-Cortez, a 28-year-old newcomer, ousted the fourth-highest-ranking Democrat in the U.S. House of Representatives, Joe Crowley.

Wow! This is big news to me for two reasons.

One, I constantly talk about how important intent is if you wish to achieve Positive Financial Karma, even as politicians stand in your way. Congratulations to Ocasio-Cortez and her followers on this front. They handily beat an entrenched incumbent who monumentally outspent her.

Two, the new Democratic nominee's economic policies are the polar opposite of mine and, I would guess, of many Americans. Among her proposals, one really caught my attention: universal job guarantees.

Now I'm not going to pretend I know all the details of this campaign promise, but I know it flies in the face of economic truths. For starters, guaranteed job security is a tempting proposal for workers, but it incentivizes giving less than one's best. After all, only tenure matters in this environment.

We have seen extreme cases where union workers get reprimand after reprimand for offenses that can be vile, but continue to draw a paycheck – which taxpayers shell out in the case of government-paid workers. That's not right, and it's also not reality. If you institutionalize guaranteed job security, you get what the former Soviet Union got for its promise to workers – shoddy work, debt-ridden corrupt government and two-hour-long bread lines.

Even the old Soviet regime has changed its tune because it can't guarantee jobs today. The economy is global and intensely competitive. Computers and manufacturing robots are commonplace, and advanced artificial intelligence and blockchain technology, a digital ledger technology for economic transactions, have arrived on the scene. There's no way all this change won't reduce the number of workers needed to do the same tasks. In their place, new technology will create a need for workers who have new skills, and competition for these jobs will be fierce because there will be fewer of them.

So what's the solution? No caring person wants to see millions of people who want to work out of work.

Government can help if they use funds to train displaced workers in new technologies. Spending money in the right places can pay taxpayers back many times over.

The second part of the job security question is personal responsibility. Make it your job to keep your job or, at the very least, to become marketable elsewhere. Individuals create their own Positive

Financial Karma by working hard and intelligently. In return, some employers will pay them equitably for their efforts, innovation and contributions.

I believe the parallel to keeping your job is staying in shape. You don't get in shape by just showing up at the gym. You have to get on the machines, break a sweat and work hard. Just as positive intent when working out will create a healthier you, positive intent in the workplace (and in school) will generate future financial rewards.

Even in a recession when you work very hard and still lose your job due to no fault of your own, your intent to better your job skills will make you marketable at perhaps a higher income elsewhere. And if you are among the growing millions of Americans who gig – who freelance for themselves or others in second and sometimes third endeavors to earn a good living – you really take your financial future in your own hands.

The so-called gig economy has featured countless individuals who worked their spare hours to create new products and services, leveraged underused skills and turned hobbies into careers. Others, who tired of depending on their employer to reward them commensurately, became full-time business owners.

I did (and continue to do) both – the side hustles and gigs, and the business of my own. Nearly 25 years ago I realized that to achieve the financial success I envisioned, I had to start my own company. Let me tell you firsthand: You can't pay yourself for just showing up when you are a business owner.

Then, over the years, I developed multiple streams of income from banking, real estate, teaching, in television and as an author. There is something to be said for having varied streams of income.

I have a client who started his own business more than 20 years ago. In the beginning, he would work 60 to 70 hours a week. Each time I would see him, he would complain that his wife would constantly ask when he was getting a full-time job with guarantees and benefits.

And then the unemployment rate spiked and companies began mass layoffs. He kept most of his clients. The economy ultimately recovered, but then sank even further two more times. Again, he kept most of his business, while friends and neighbors lost their income because they depended on others. His wife finally stopped asking him to find a "full-time job."

The moral of the story? In the end, you are what you make of yourself. Ultimately, you create Positive Financial Karma with hard work, focused study and sometimes monumental efforts. That's your guarantee.

Free College

A number of politicians are jumping on the free college bandwagon. Taxpayers, hold on to your wallets!

Taking a page from the Bernie Sanders playbook, some states want to offer free community college – New Jersey being one of the latest. Sanders is a socialist and a socialist's view of the world is to spend everybody else's money. Sounds great on the campaign trail, but in the case of my home state, we are already overtaxed and in poor financial condition. Almost a dozen other states offer some version of free community college, from California and New York to Kentucky and Tennessee. The problem is that here in New Jersey, the spending spigot has been stuck "on" my entire adult life.

Policies like this chase financially successful people and companies out of the state, which New Jersey can ill afford because it is already among the nation's leaders in residents migrating out of state. I see this firsthand as clients continually ask me about the tax implications of leaving New Jersey.

The most disturbing aspect of this trend is, rich or poor, people don't want to leave, but feel they must. The wealthy have the means to migrate and they can simply move. On the other hand, middle- and lower-income taxpayers can't afford to stay but many don't have the means to pack up and leave. They don't have as simple a choice as wealthier taxpayers do. It's a shame because it doesn't have to be this way.

The outflow from New Jersey has been steady for a while. As individuals and corporations continue to leave, who will pay for these and other government dictates? Someone has to pay for "free" college – and we can certainly have a discussion about the cost of higher education being completely out of control. But free college on the backs of taxpayers isn't the answer. This is just bad fiscal policy – and a misnomer.

There is no such thing as free college.

Someone will pay for it, so let's call it what it is – another taxpayer burden.

Here's one alternative: Make students perform workfare, even if it is in the form of community service, instead of receiving welfare in the form of free tuition. Give them the opportunity to contribute and develop their Positive Financial Karma. Let them put skin in the game by providing a service and receiving some form of compensation.

If they need to take out loans, they won't be the first to do so. College debt should not overwhelm students and their parents, but asking students to make a modest investment in their future isn't heartless. And there is help that doesn't burden taxpayers so much. For example, some federal programs forgive debt for teaching in areas that need teachers. Debt forgiveness employee benefits are also becoming increasingly popular in private industry. I have a client whose daughter dropped out of college three weeks after he paid a nonrefundable tuition. She found herself, went back to school, got lost again and left him holding a tuition bill for zero credits again.

Fast forward 10 years when she's married and has kids. She goes back to school part-time while working and parenting, paying sane state tuition. She gets her BA and then decides to get a MA in teaching. She takes out a reasonable amount of debt, pays the rest and now earns a good salary.

It's a cliché, but where there's a will there's a way. My client's daughter found a way and is now thriving, having achieved some measure of Positive Financial Karma. Paying for higher education may not be easy, but it can be done without taxpayer-paid, "free" tuition. For those who work hard and sacrifice to earn their degrees and a decent living, their financial karma can only be positive.

The Wall

Immigration is the question and the "Wall" may be one of the answers.

But the Wall is not the only answer, a be-all, end-all solution to illegal immigration. Sensible immigration policy is. Let me explain, and please hold the tomatoes until the end of the chapter.

From day one as he campaigned for the presidency of the United States, Donald Trump promised to build a wall to separate most of Mexico and the United States. Thanks to the president's insistent call, this partition has become more famous than the previous most famous one, Pink Floyd's album, "The Wall." I'm guessing he will accept nothing less in any immigration package.

All kidding aside, little in this country produces as much emotion as this still-to-be-built-if-ever structure. And that's the problem. Emotion is standing in the way of logic, which is the only way two sides with starkly different views on immigration and national security can ever come to any sort of compromise.

So let's take the emotion out of this discussion and discard the politics that come with the subject. There's enough blame to go around for both political parties, given that the United States hasn't really had an immigration policy in my lifetime. As with most things, Congress plays kick the can as our country's immigration challenges become more ingrained. Illegal immigration is a result of Washington's inaction – which, remember, is still an action – and only our Congressional representatives can fix this problem.

A focal point of any immigration legislation has to be sensible security and a process by which people can come to this country legally. Let's face it, virtually every immigrant comes here for a better economic future, a better life.

My father was an immigrant from Italy, coming to the United States when he was 11 years old. He spoke no English and had to fend for himself in many ways. My father never complained about the difficulties and was always grateful he had the chance to become an American. He often felt he had experienced the best of both worlds: Although poor while growing up in Italy, he was rich in culture and family.

My father was processed at Ellis Island in 1951. He worked hard to get an education and a career and was a contributing member of society. He then grabbed hold of the opportunity for upward mobility in the United States by obtaining advanced educational degrees and climbing into the middle class – the American dream. He also did it legally. We were and remain today a nation of laws. When people don't like a law, there is a process to change it. Until then, we must follow the laws in place.

Certainly, there are ways to make it to and in America today, even under current law. Many companies, for example, depend on immigrants – illegal and legal – to survive. Why not match would-be immigrants with companies whose survival depends on these immigrants to fill their jobs? We're not only talking about farming and other labor positions that just don't have enough American citizens to fill them, but about technical jobs in places like Silicon Valley filled by immigrants from around the world with math and science degrees.

Immigration isn't bad, but it's a mess as it stands now. So let's look at some solutions.

We can put the onus on companies to vet their workforce to ensure they aren't employing undocumented immigrants. The problem here is that many illegal aliens have documents – fake documents. Are we going to pile more regulation on top of the over-regulation business owners continue to face? In the interest of fairness, fixing immigration isn't the job of business.

Maybe we can structure a program that provides temporary workers who return to their countries when their jobs are completed. We need the workers and the workers need the jobs, so this is a perfect match. Ultimately, any process should match up people who are willing to work where we need workers. This could be one part of the solution.

Another part of the solution is to fix the temporary visa program. We lose far too many students and foreign workers who enter our country this way and never return to their home countries or renew their work visas.

The foundation of any solution has to be a sane immigration policy, once and for all, which admits a set number of immigrants each year, fully vetted in a best attempt to protect our citizens.

Those immigrants who fill the jobs most in need would receive priority. This isn't a black- or brown-and-white issue. It's about choosing a person or families of any color who want to improve their lot and are willing and able to work hard to accomplish their dreams.

Finally, we need to have some sort of wall. It can be a wall of mortar and steel, a wall of technology, a wall of people or a well-thought-out combination of these and other approaches. Protect our citizens not only from gang members who may try to cross the border, however many or few they are, but also from would-be terrorists, who can come from around the world to cross through porous northern and southern borders in an attempt to do harm to the United States. The idea of America having no borders is not just a bad idea, it's absurd.

Let's establish from the start that we are all in favor of children and families trying to make better lives, and that we don't care about race or creed. Then, let's create a logical and thoughtful immigration policy in which we all become winners. In this way, we can turn what has been decidedly negative karma into Positive Financial Karma for all.

No News, Bad News

If you're old enough to remember, there used to be a wide choice of newspapers to read. In New York City alone you had a choice of more than a half-dozen daily papers. You would ride the subways and see half of the straphangers reading a folded newspaper with one hand. To finish your day, you would turn to one of the three major broadcast networks and listen to a news anchor that almost everyone trusted. Few people questioned the veracity of the news or those who delivered it, at least compared to today.

Fast forward to now. A wave of technology — from cable to social media to streaming handheld devices — has almost drowned the newspaper industry, delivering news, noise and entertainment on demand, 24/7. Newspapers continue to disappear and those that survive do so with a robust online presence. Millennials and even Gen Xers get their information via handheld devices. As a college professor, I can tell you that my students get most of their information this way.

Perhaps the biggest change over the years is the definition of the news. We tend to read publications and watch shows that align with our beliefs. So we think that's the real news. The information providers we don't like are the "fake news." On the other side of the coin, media outlets are presenting the news to align with the audience that supports them with ratings. The result is that the truth simply becomes a matter of convenience (and advertising dollars). Too often, this divide is triggered by politics, if not by politicians themselves.

Quite often, cable news channels cover the same story at the same time. I tried an experiment that you should also undertake. I set my remote control to switch with one click between news stations with differing points of view. I was amazed by what I discovered. Two networks covering the exact same story with polar opposite descriptions of the details. How could this be? This would be like watching two competing weather channels with one saying it's sunny in Philadelphia and the other saying it's raining. So you call a friend in Philadelphia to ask what the weather is like, and you learn there were sun showers. You then discover that the reason each station presented the forecast that way was because the majority of their respective viewers wanted a specific type of weather that day in Philadelphia. Crazy, right?

My point is while the newspapers, television stations and radio news outlets that adapt to today's information consumer will survive, fake news should not. This is basic karma. If people present fake news, you expect it to come back to bite them. They're committing fraud, and that usually never ends well. Mass information fraud is a particular problem because so many people pick up on it like it is true. This happens to everyone – left, right and center of political persuasions.

So what do you do to find truth when you still want accurate information?

In today's environment, when we are led to believe every person with a social media account is a reporter, believe nothing that you hear and only half of what you see. Find the time to read a newspaper or listen to a news show from the "other side" and compare it to how "your side" presents the news. Often, you would think they live in alternate realities, but at least you're listening to both sides. As President Reagan said of the old Soviet Union when they agreed to reduce their nuclear arsenals, "Trust, but verify."

I teach various auditing courses to accounting majors and the results are always about verifying. If, for example, you believe in cryptocurrency like bitcoin and you see positive articles about it without challenging your own beliefs or verifying what you read, you could buy swampland.

Verifying is critical to investing and finance in general, and to your Positive Financial Karma.

And, if you don't believe in verifying, I'll harken back to the glory days of newspapers and say, "If you believe that, I have a bridge in Brooklyn I'd like to sell you."

When Consumers
Fight Back

NFL Flag Protest

During the 2017-18 season, players around the National Football League (NFL) protested against a variety of what they believed were societal woes by kneeling or raising their fists during the playing of the national anthem. This continued the next season, although with fewer participants.

As with most arguments in an increasingly divided country, no amount of talk was going to resolve this issue. Those against believed these actions disrespected the flag, our country and our veterans. Those in favor believed that problems in primarily minority communities had been ignored for too long.

To see injustice in society and then act to correct it is something we should not only support, but be part of. Martin Luther King, Jr.'s commitment to non-violent protests in the 1960s ultimately played a part in the election of President Barack Obama some 40 years later. What an awesome example of cause and effect! Will the NFL protests have the same impact sometime in the future? We may not know for a very long time.

Most reasonable people can agree that the players' concerns about injustice should be addressed. The question becomes whether the method and timing of their protests are appropriate. If you break it down, the players are employees who are protesting during their time at work. If their employers are OK with that, then by all means proceed. But like any other business, the NFL has customers that may have a different point of view, and I have said all along that the fans will ultimately decide how this plays out.

I'm an accountant so I will focus on the money and not the social aspect of this. If you don't like something, say so with your wallet. This time-tested method of protest has a long history. Now, consumers on both sides of the political aisle have weaponized it. Organized boycotts of companies advertising on shows of both conservative and liberal commentators have financially hurt the outlets that carry them. You need only look at how the forces behind gun control affected the sponsors of the National Rifle Association (NRA). The greatest threat to the NRA's effectiveness and even its very existence are not marches or rallies, but economic boycotts of its advertising supporters.

What boycotts like these have shown is the power a group of American consumers can wield. In the NFL that power comes from the fans. In one corner you have the average fan who watches on television, goes to an occasional game (at exorbitant prices) and buys jerseys and NFL products (at exorbitant prices). In the other corner you have wealthy owners and players. They both fill their wallets, but the fans can put a stop to this.

In 2017, the little people hurt a billion-dollar business with their brand of "economic sanctions." They stayed away from games and turned their TVs to other stations. They stopped buying NFL-branded products. When advertisers suffer, either the owners and players change or you'll see the continuation of some really nasty financial karma.

The NFL and its protesting players can find a solution if they try.

First, the players and owners can come to terms on how to collectively address the injustices in our society, which would include a financial commitment from both sides. Next, they can provide incentives to draw fans back to supporting their favorite teams and the sport. If these steps are successful, the NFL would once again prosper financially as a result of its intention to help society.

Now that's Positive Financial Karma!

Your Opinion, My Dime

Ok, I'll admit it. I am a huge Bruce Springsteen fan. He has had a very positive effect on my life, especially his deeply personal autobiography. I listen to his albums and I'm proud to call him a fellow New Jerseyan. I respect his right to freely voice his opinions, whether or not I agree with what he says.

But Bruce, please don't get on a soapbox on my dime.

Springsteen starred in a recent one-man Broadway show in which he talked about his life and the songs that frame it. I saw the show and he was great, as always. This guy is a national treasure. But at another performance he called a timeout and gave his decidedly opposition views on the immigration crisis and separating children from their parents who had entered the country illegally.

People paid a lot of money to see him on Broadway. A quick glance at available tickets online showed few tickets were under $1,000. Among the legion of Bruce fans are supporters of President Trump. They didn't pay these exorbitant ticket prices to hear Bruce's political views. He gave his views anyway, and he isn't the only celebrity to do so.

The night before Bruce went off script, lead singer Eddie Vedder of Pearl Jam went off on Trump and his administration's immigration policy during a concert in London. There was likely a smaller percentage of Trump supporters in London than in New York, but that is beside the point. I had the same problem with this outburst as I did with Springsteen's impromptu speech – please give it in another forum.

I understand people have strong, negative feelings about President Trump. That's their right, and it is also their right to express it. But please do so in the proper forum. Write a song, a blog or an op-ed in a newspaper, call a news conference, do a podcast, do something – anything else – to voice your opinion at the appropriate time and place.

People want to see entertainers for the entertainment. They pay top dollar to see Broadway shows and concerts. They shell out more for music and t-shirts and other products connected to their favorite entertainers. They are not, however, going to these expensive events to hear political opinions. Giving political speeches polarizes entertainers' fans just as it does in society. It also creates negative financial karma because it leaves people feeling isolated and leads to buyer's remorse.

So Bruce, if you read this, please don't drag your fans into the deep swamps of divisive politics when they pay to hear you sing about the swamps of Jersey. Play the songs and tell the stories your fans love, and exercise your right to political free speech in another venue.

The Boss

In the previous chapter, I was a bit critical of Bruce Springsteen, so in fairness I want to provide another view of "The Boss" – a more positive one.

I can really identify with Bruce. He is from New Jersey. I'm from New Jersey. Bruce is Italian (in part). I'm Italian. Bruce is from humble beginnings and became an international superstar, and I'm from humble beginnings. Oh well, close enough.

I never met Bruce (no need for last names) and I don't feel I need to. The closest I've been to him is in the second row of his Broadway show, about 12 feet from him. He shared some powerful energy with me that night and over the years – at concerts, on the radio and in his book. I'm grateful for the positive vibration I received when I saw him and feel motivated to provide the same positive vibe to my clients, those who see me on television and, for that matter, anyone I come in contact with.

I have friends who were lifelong Bruce fans who now refuse to listen to his music because of his political views. I'm not one of them. Whether I agree or disagree with Bruce's politics is of no consequence. In fact, I don't care what anyone's politics are except if they run for office. It's unfortunate that political divisiveness now affects what music some people will listen to, but I will not allow politics to cut me off from things I enjoy.

Great music, even if it is only a three- or four-minute song, has a way of inspiring. Great music can make us believe we can realize our dreams. I find Bruce's music, deeply rooted in the struggle to achieve the American dream, very inspiring. Bruce's chances of making the big time were no greater than the average person's, but he did make it, and no one handed him a thing. He willed himself to success with an unrelenting drive and the desire to give his audience all he had every single night. The boomerang effect of this intention is that he now has wealth and fame, while he appears to remain grounded.

His story is one of Positive Financial Karma.

Pay to Play

For a good part of my adult life, I have watched while the National Collegiate Athletic Association (NCAA) rakes in increasingly obscene amounts of money via advertisers, ticket sales, merchandise and television rights related to their major sports programs. At the same time, players and schools continue to make news by accepting illegal compensation – illegal because the NCAA makes it so.

I'm a fan of free markets, but not of free work and labor.

Pay the players, NCAA! They contribute mightily to your growing financial fortunes.

This, like equal pay in the workplace, is about fairness. A lot of people, quite frankly, make tons of money off "student-athletes" whose families often struggle financially. None of the students currently get a piece of the very large pie – at least not publicly – but they should be paid something.

We hear stories about famous college athletes taking under-the-table payments from boosters and who knows who else. This seems to be increasingly common. When you hear what college athletes get under the table, it's not exactly life-changing amounts of money. This NCAA-forbidden practice needs to end, and it will when college athletes are compensated for their work.

Why not come in out of the dark, NCAA, and treat your athletes fairly? Let those who contribute the most to your financial success enjoy the same compensation-for-contribution that any employee of any other business expects. You wouldn't have to pay them incredible compensation, but enough so that they don't feel forced to accept "illegal" payments or declare early for the pros because of poor financial conditions.

I believe this issue will come to a head sooner rather than later. Maybe it happens because the NCAA will begin to feel public or political pressure to pay their athletes something. I don't know the formula, but it should be appropriate for each school.

If the NCAA doesn't change its mind on this issue, will the players go on strike? Maybe not nationwide, due to the enormous logistical feat needed to accomplish it, but I can see players from individual schools withholding their services. I do know that the NCAA, as a nonprofit, doesn't pay a nickel's worth of tax on its enormous profits.

Frankly, this is a joke.

Do the players unionize? The courts shot down this idea a few years ago when Northwestern University athletes attempted it.

At some point, the colleges making the most money from their sports programs may allow players to share in some of the wealth because of public opinion, the courts or continued scandal.

Maybe a Congressional threat of stripping the NCAA of its nonprofit status will force college sports' governing body to finally reward its employees – and employees are what the players are.

Change is needed in a system where players create all the wealth but can't share in the bounty. This is simply a matter of fairness. It's a matter of giving everyone the opportunity to achieve Positive Financial Karma.

Term Limits

If you read the previous chapters, you know by now that I believe we need term limits for elected officials at every level of government: federal, state and local.

I know the argument against term limits. Opponents argue that we already have limits because we can vote anyone out of office. But term limits would offer a system of checks and balances. We can't blame the politicians who remain in office for decades when we keep reelecting them. We get the government we deserve. But we should strive to demand more from our elected officials.

I think it's honorable that people want to serve in government to try to make things better, and that most politicians start with good intentions. I know some very fine people who serve in government, and I know they are there to do the right thing by those they represent. And they seem to conclude that the best thing for their constituents is for the same politicians to keep winning re-election. This is when "re-electionism" strikes and becomes the primary focus of most politicians.

That's why we need term limits. If you want to serve, that's great. But understand it will only be for a finite period of time. If you want to continue to serve, no problem – run for another position.

There is no reason we can't have term limits. Congress limits any one president to two terms, but strangely will not put term limits on senators and representatives. Why is that? I think the answer is quite clear – politicians don't want to limit their own power. "We the people" need to do that for them.

Without fail, members of Congress continually have the lowest job approval rating of anyone, yet they don't typically have a problem getting re-elected. This happens by virtue of being in office term after term and building significant re-election war chests along with an army of loyalists with a vested interest in their campaign success. These factors make the system one-sided and unfair.

The system is broken. Term limits are not the sole solution, but they should be part of one.

Vote!

Please, vote.

It's an incredible privilege to vote, an action some citizens around the world take at great peril when they literally risk their lives for the opportunity to wait on line for days to vote in a free election. On our own shores, voting should remind us of the countless Americans who gave their lives to afford us the chance to select our government.

I make a concerted effort to vote in every election, whether it is for the presidency, the local school board or everything in between. You should, too. It makes no difference who you vote for – just vote. I have voted for Democrats, Republicans and Independents based upon who I thought was most qualified to represent me.

When I vote, I think about how President George Washington warned our young nation in his farewell address to avoid excessive political party spirit. In today's vernacular, he might have said, "Don't place loyalty to party above loyalty to country." Clearly, we haven't listened very well given the current state of our nation.

Voting (or not) and karma are interconnected. By strict definition, karma means action that triggers a corresponding reaction. But in this case, inaction also creates a karmic effect – and maybe not the effect you intended. If you don't vote, you allow others to choose your government for you. If you're happy with the choices others make for you, great. But if you would like to see things change, if you want improvement, if you think we are still less than perfect, then vote.

You have the ability to influence outcomes – the direction of your local, state and federal governments – so you should use that power and vote. Government has a lot of say in our everyday lives. Why remain an onlooker when it comes to selecting the people who make the laws we must follow?

Don't be a spectator. Be an active participant. Voting is literally ground zero when it comes to creating Positive Financial Karma.